W9-DJK-092

FINDING & KEEPING CUSTOMERS:

A Small Business Handbook

by
H. GREGORY
Pinstripe Publishing

WARNER MEMORIAL LIBRARY
EASTERN COLLEGE
ST. DAVIDS, PA. 19087

7-21-89

FINDING & KEEPING CUSTOMERS:
A Small Business Handbook
by H.Gregory

HF 5415.5 .G75 1989
Gregory, H.
Finding & keeping customers

© Copyright 1988 by Helen I. Gregory

ALL RIGHTS RESERVED. No part of this book may be reproduced or transmitted in any form or by any means, electronic or mechanical, including photocopying, recording, or by any information storage or retrieval system without written permission from the author EXCEPT for the inclusion of brief quotations in a review.

First published: March, 1989

Published by: **PINSTRIPE PUBLISHING**
                    Post Office Box 711
                    Sedro-Woolley, WA 98284
                    U.S.A.

ISBN 0-941973-02-6
Library of Congress Catalog Card Number: 88-92699

The majority of illustrations in this book are from Humorous Office Spot Illustrations designed by Bob Censoni and published by DOVER PUBLICATIONS, INC., New York. Used by permission.

Manufactured in the United States of America

CONTENTS

Foreword.. v

Acknowledgments................................. vii

A Word from the Author.......................... viii

Section One: Preparation........................ 1

Product knowledge...5
Personal knowledge...8
Personal appearance...8
Wardrobe planning...9
Color analysis...13
Voice analysis...15
Body language...17
Attitude...19
Paying your dues...23
Goal setting...25
Money, mathematics, & goals...29
The ears have it!...30
Writing the sales presentation...31
Handling objections...39
Practice! Practice! Practice!...39
Summary...41

Section Two: Finding Customers 43

Identifying your customer...45
Finding your customer...46
Qualifying your customer...51
Drop in customers...52
Making appointments...54
Making the call...57
Giving the sales presentation...61
Do's & Don't's of presentation...67
Summary...70

Section Three: Keeping Customers............... 71

Presentation follow up...74
The follow up system...77
Customer service...82
Handling customer complaints...91
Summary...98

Appendix... 99

Resources...101
Library Research Guide...113
Eleven Ways to create profit-making advertising...121
Follow up suggestions for some businesses...123
The press release...129
Making newsletters...135
The business cycle...139

Index... 141

FOREWORD

Marketing master Stanley Marcus, who turned Neiman-Marcus into a national institution, tells entrepreneurs , "I found that when I took care of customers extremely well, and made them a focal point, profit inevitably flowed from that."

Sounds obvious to me, but is anybody paying attention? Although I am a business owner and deal with customers on a daily basis myself, I am keenly aware that when I'm on the other side being the customer I am seldom treated with respect—or even common courtesy.

What's going on here? It seems topsy-turvy to me. Large companies frequently pay enormous salaries and fees to those people who are in charge of finding customers. Often as not, however, those people on the front lines, the ones who deal directly with the customer, are poorly paid, undertrained, and regularly replaced. While that may not excuse the poor treatment we receive as customers, it does explain it.

We laugh when we hear television's Basil Fawlty announce, "Innkkeeping would be a lovely occupation if it wasn't for the bloody guests." But when we encounter Basil Fawltys in real life, there's nothing amusing about it at all.

Large companies, alas, are not the only ones at fault here. Budding entrepreneurs frequently fall in love with their product or service, but fail to consider that their success ultimately depends on customers, those people who have chosen to do business with them.

How can we learn to make customers our focal point? This book is a superb starting place. It will carry you a long way in mastering the basics that will make your business a standout.

It is also helpful to become conscious of the ways in which you are attracted to doing business with other companies. When was the last time you received superb service? I am willing to guess that you were so pleased (and astonished) that you probably told all of your friends.

A telephone call I made to L.L.Bean is one of my

favorite memories. When a dress I wanted to order was dropped from their catalog, their customer service person located the remaining stock and discovered that they still had several in my size. Of course, they got my order!

"Men and women who market their services to the best advantage must recognize that the relationship between employers and employees will be more in the nature of a partnership consisting of the employer, the employee, and the public they serve. Both the employer and employee are employed by the public. If they fail to serve well, they pay by their loss of the privilege of serving."

Those words were written by Napoleon Hill in his classic success book, *Think and Grow Rich*. It's a philosophy shared by Paul Hawken, the young man who is largely responsible for starting the health food industry and runs Smith & Hawken.

"The market is as much a part of your company as you are," believes Hawken. "After all, it represents one-half of the ledger. To succeed, your business must earn the permission of the marketplace. The customer must give your business permission to sell to him. I firmly believe that no concept is more important to an entrepreneur."

Hill and Hawken have taken a position that is shared by few. But those companies who value their customers and consider them partners in success, become the exception that customers rave about. They also become the companies that grow, prosper, and stay in business year after year after year.

--Barbara J. Winter

Barbara J. Winter is a writer, newsletter producer, and small business workshop leader. Write to her at MAKING THINGS HAPPEN, P.O.Box 35412, Minneapolis, MN 55435 for more information about her newsletters and workshops.

ACKNOWLEDGMENTS

A special thanks to the many kind folks who contributed in one way or another to the worthiness of this book.

To **Barbara J. Winter**, for taking time from her busy schedule to prepare the Foreword, to **June Cornett**, for providing insight into the Chamber of Commerce, to **Robert Serling**, for sharing his "Eleven Ways to Create Profit-Making Advertising," and to **Dover Publications**, whose Humorous Office Illustrations provide comic relief throughout the text.

Thanks also to good friends, former employers, and the gracious and patient librarians at the **Skagit Valley Community College Library**, the **Sedro-Woolley Library**, and the **King County Library System**, as well as the following, who proffered information on associations, books, magazines, and newsletters so necessary to the small business movement:

Barbara Brabec, The National Home Business Report, **Sylvia Campbell-Landman**, Pairs, **Matthew C. Carr**, The Business Owner, **John M. Christensen**, Independent Computer Consultants Association, **Charlie & Jan Fletcher**, Home Business Advisor and New Families, **Steven Fletcher**, Shoestring Marketer Newsletter, **Joanne R. Frank**, Business Network, **Janet H. Hutson**, Handweavers Guild of America, **Kate Kelly**, The Publicity Manual, **Betty Crawford** of McGraw-Hill Book Company, **Susan A. Kesten**, Success Magazine, **Barney Kingston**, Opportunity Magazine, **Thomas H. Latimer** of the American Federation of Small Business, **Hannah C. McGarity**, Working at Home, **Jane L. Melton** of the American Association for Adult and Continuing Education, **William H. Prouty** of the Perfect Life Connection, **Rosemary Souder** of Triad Publications for Payment in Full, **Dottie Walters**, Never Underestimate the Selling Power of a Woman, and **James L. Young** of the National Writers Club.

To these and any I may have missed, my sincere appreciation for your contribution in this effort.

--Helen Gregory

A WORD FROM THE AUTHOR...

I've been around small business for a lot of years. My Dad owned his own business. (He let me do his typing.)

My very best jobs were in small businesses, from entry-level clerk-cashier to Office Manager to Comptroller. Those years of gainful employment taught me a great deal--about consumer credit, the small loan process, how to organize paperwork and people, how to keep inventories, handle government regulations, payroll, accounts receivable, accounts payable, tax reports, detailed accounting, and office management. By the time I was ready for my own business, I had "comptrolled" everything from financial statements to toilet paper--and learned that sometimes there wasn't much difference!

Self employment brings other lessons to be learned. Since no fellow-merchant would share any methods of survival with me, I studied a multitude of small business books, magazines, and pamphlets. Most were addressing the Wonders of Wall Street, the upwardly mobile youngsters who possessed capital and connections to reach $500,000 in sales their first year in business.

Me? I was struggling to pay the rent! Where was the sage advice for those of us reaching for a modest share? For me, it came in bits and pieces along the way. From between-the-lines study of those books and magazines, from good friends, from past experience working for someone else, from scaled down advice tossed around by the big-business experts, and a lot from trial-and-error.

May that experience shorten your pathway to success in small business. (And may all your financial statements be found in the Record Book and not in the outhouse.)

--Helen Gregory

SECTION ONE: PREPARE!

Product knowledge

Personal knowledge

Personal appearance

Wardrobe planning

Color analysis

Voice analysis

Body language

Attitude

Paying your dues

Goal setting

Money, mathematics, & goals

The ears have it!

Writing the sales presentation

Handling objections

Practice! Practice! Practice!

Summary

WARNING! DISCLAIMER!

This book isn't about finding a suitable product or business. It assumes you have already made that choice, and hopefully, one that fills a need.

It does address preparing yourself and your product knowledge for finding and keeping customers. Those customers may be clients, patients, students, or anyone who does business with you on a repeat basis. That customer might be either male or female, and no intentional slight against either is intended in this book by the use of the pronouns **he** and **she.**

Your business might be that of owning a retail shop, wholesale supplier, door to door selling, or multilevel marketing, selling either products or services. Any of these could be homebased or managed from a commercial location.

Although extensive research was done in compiling the information herein, the author and publisher assume no responsibility for errors, inaccuracies, omissions, or any other inconsistency. This book is by no means a substitute for professional or legal advice, and no guarantee of success is implied or given. Any slights against persons or organizations are unintentional.

WARNING! DISCLAIMER!

Business is a game of hide-and-seek: customers hide, and you must seek them out. Before you begin that search, however, there are some things you must do to prepare yourself.

You must arm yourself with intimate knowledge not only of your product, but also that of your competition. What are its strengths? What are its weaknesses? How can your product better serve the customer?

You'll need to develop a good image, not only for your customer, but also for yourself. You must dress, move, and speak in a manner that promotes your product and your business in the best possible regard.

You must create a sales presentation that is delivered in articulate style, that motivates your customer to buy, and that promotes confidence in you and in your product.

Preparation is your countdown in this game of hide-and-seek. It is what keeps you from looking in all the wrong places. It is what makes you able to sell and serve your customers once you find them.

So count carefully and thoroughly. The time to start is now!

Preparation is the countdown in the hide-and-seek game of business.

PRODUCT KNOWLEDGE

It's been said that "knowledge is power." Product knowledge--knowing and believing in your product--is the power that will fill you with self confidence, and that confidence will win respect and patronage from your customers.

You must know far more about your product than the average person. Why? Because customers will turn to you for answers. They will expect you to be an expert on your subject, and will come to you with their questions. Without the answers, you will lose credibility and future sales and referrals, and, just possibly, your business.

How do you begin to learn? A good place to start is to try the product yourself!

Use it. Abuse it. Tear it apart! If you can't believe in it after tearing it apart, or trying to, then maybe your first lesson is that you have the wrong product. You must believe in your product before you can sell it to someone else. Is it something you would share with a friend--like a new restaurant in town that you tried and loved? Things we have tried and enjoyed we share with our friends. It is no different with your business.

You want to experience ahead of time what your customer will find. When using the product yourself, make a list of questions and comments as they come to mind. Know the components or ingredients, and how they are better than the competition's. Analyze deeply, finding any and all objections you are likely to hear, and then begin your search for the answers BEFORE your customer asks you!

You may think you have all the answers if you're selling a product you manufacture yourself--it's easy to become too familiar with such things. But wait! You can and should make a few samples and test the market. Have your friends and relatives and coworkers try out the product and report their findings back to you. You'll find there are a few questions you didn't think of! But they'll need answers prepared.

If you're not selling a self-manufactured product, the first place to seek information is from your supplier, manufacturer, or sales leader. Attend

5

meetings. Ask for literature--sales brochures and pamphlets--and study them. The information you will find in these brochures and pamphlets will surely stress the benefits of your product. Indeed they should! And you will need to be aware of those benefits when writing your sales presentation (covered later in this section).

Don't be satisfied studying benefits only. Continue to investigate, outside of these sources. Where? Your competition is a good place to start!

Contact them with a twofold purpose in mind: to obtain product information, and to watch how they give the sales presentation. Listen to what they have to say, collect their pamphlets and brochures. Note the benefits that they stress and any limits they feel apply to your product. A word of caution here: this is an investigative and learning procedure for you. Your purpose is not to convert them to nor defend your product, but to gain insight into what you will be up against, and what answers you must prepare for your own sales presentation.

Ask questions. Investigate the product. Offer objections and listen carefully to the responses you get. How do they "turn around" your objection? Did you feel threatened or pressured? Was it a comfortable presentation?

Thank them for their time and information, saying that you'll consider what they have offered and let them know next Tuesday (or some specific day next week). This will help your exit, or theirs, without pressure to buy the product, and you will indeed telephone them on the day specified to say that after careful consideration you have decided not to purchase so-and-so. Now! Watch how they handle that! If you have made contact with some real "pros," you have some valuable training to note.

Having scouted the competition and tested your product yourself, your notebook should be full of questions to resolve. Next stop: the Public Library.

Check the card-catalog or microfiche under "subject matter" for publications pertaining to your product--its benefits and its limits. Trade magazines, publications aimed at a particular type of business, are also found at the library. Ask the librarian to help you find them. Look for ones that will offer something relevant to your business/product.

For example, gift stores subscribe to magazines about new giftwares and marketing in their field; apparel stores subscribe to magazines offering the future in fashion; health food stores pick the ones announcing the newest in nutrition news and new products available, and so on.

In addition to product research, you might locate a few books on selling and marketing while you are there. Check the Appendix in this book for suggestions as well

In the books that you find and study, also make note of titles and authors listed in the bibliography that may apply to your search for information. Keep in mind that you must sufficiently know both the good and the bad in order to pass your customer's test!

There is no set length of time for your research into product knowledge, but you should know up front that research is time consuming. The more time spent, the better and more thorough your search. Spend at least two hours each time you study. This can be daily, weekly, or whatever time you have or can assign. If you are serious about your business, you will allot a regular time to building it, and never waiver from that time. You _are_ "working!"

You will, at some point, reach utter confusion in your research. That is the time to put your notes away in a safe place for a few days. You'll pull them out later, to organize before writing your sales presentation.

Meanwhile, it's time to begin work on yourself!

"My problem lies in reconciling my gross habits with my net income."
                    Errol Flynn (1909-1959)

PERSONAL KNOWLEDGE

How well do you know yourself? How objective are you? How do you come across to others? You may not be what you think you are--very often your friends will not tell you what they really think of you. Either they don't want to hurt your feelings--a commendable trait--or they are jealous of your qualities and don't want to admit it to you or to themselves!

How can you really tell? You must be very objective. You must study your appearance, voice, body language, and attitude as if they belonged to someone else--to someone you might do business with.

To be objective doesn't mean only to criticize; you undoubtedly have good qualities that can be capitalized on even more! Allowing that, and improving where necessary on your shortcomings, you can develop good self-esteem and good self-confidence.

Where do you start? With a little research, a full length mirror, and a tape recorder!

PERSONAL APPEARANCE

The first thing a potential customer will notice is your appearance. From the shine on your hair to the shine on your shoes, without saying a word, your customer receives the image of who or what you are. First impressions can make the difference between getting and not getting the sale.

Your total appearance is your uniform, so to speak, and we all know that the "uniform is ninety percent of the job!" It is especially true in law enforcement. And, would the Superior Court Judge command equal respect on the bench without his robes? How about a group of young men playing

> *"Nothing succeeds like the appearance of success."*
>
> *Christopher Lasch*

football on the field? We know they are having fun, yet put those young men into padded, colorful uniforms and helmets, and we realize they are a force to be reckoned with. We respect them more, because they are in uniform.

There is also a uniform of wealth in our society. Allbeit unspoken or unwritten, when you dress and conduct yourself as a weathly person, you command respect and the RIGHT TO MAKE MONEY! People like to deal with successful people!

Whether you are short or tall, round-of-figure or pencil thin, you can and must dress professionally for your job.

Your research might start in the Public Library or local book store. There are many good books on "dressing for success." (Check Appendix in this book for suggestions).

Another place to research is television. Watch the commercials. What are they selling? How are they dressed? What colors are they wearing--neutral shades of grays, beiges, or whites? Or bright colors?

Bright colors attract the eye, and may distract from the product. But they have their place.

The basic rule is to be conservative in dress and groomed in personal hygiene. You want to attract respect, not merely attention! Think of yourself as an advertisement for what you are selling, and plan your wardrobe accordingly.

WARDROBE PLANNING

A tailored business suit is never in bad taste (unless it is TOO tailored to your confirmation). It doesn't have to be a blue serge or charcoal pinstripe, but should be a non-offensive basic hue that flatters your complexion (more on color analysis later). For women, a skirted suit is the uniform for business, and may be in one of your "power" colors. Keep blouses and shirts in a light neutral tone, whites and beiges, or pale pastels, and conservative ties for men. Of course the acceptable business wardrobe can vary, according the product you are selling.

If you are selling sporting goods and wear, your uniform will be an outfit from the line you sell. Watch out for the shorts--they are offensive to some! Same goes for swim suits! Just because you sell them doesn't mean you have to wear them in the store--that's what mannequins are for!

A massive wardrobe is not necessary to look respectable every business day. Aside from the basics of underwear, hosiery, a light raincoat, an umbrella, and an attache' case if needed, your wardrobe plan will start with two tailored suits, one in a dark basic color, the other in a light, neutral color. They needn't be the same style or fabric. Next you'll want two blouses or shirts, one white and tailored, the other in a light color and a bit dressier--striped for men, dressier fabric for women. You'll need two pair of shoes (medium height heel for women), one pair in a dark basic color to go with your dark suit, and the other pair in a neutral medium shade, to wear with your lighter suit. Keep hosiery in neutral to dark tones, to blend with your hem line and shoes. If you want people to look at your feet, wear white hosiery and white shoes! Light and bright colors attract the eye.

Women will want a moderate size handbag in a neutral shade and conservative style that will fit any occasion. Men might want a hat. Fabrics that best promote an air of success are natural ones--wool, silk, and cotton. For handbags, attache' cases, and shoes, stick to real leather.

Accessories should be carefully considered when planning your business uniform. These include jewelry, pocket handkerchiefs, neckties, scarves, handbags, flowers, hairclips, hats, and the like. A dash of color can be added to your uniform with a necktie or silk scarf, and will help keep the customer's attention drawn to your head and face area, making eye contact a bit easier.

Jewelry can distract from your message when overdone. Unless you are in jewelry sales, wear only three pieces at a time, not counting your wedding rings. For example, men might choose a clever tie tack, a handsome wristwatch, and a nice solid ring or lapel pin. Women might choose a pair of earrings (count as one piece of jewelry), a coordinating necklace or brooch, and a bracelet or ring.

For men, gold or silver neckchains can be worn under the shirt during business engagements, and women can keep anklebracelets inside a handbag.

If you have been awarded with lapel pins for merit or product knowledge, count them as jewelry but wear them proudly! They serve as silent proof that you are serious about your profession, and silent sales tools to the customer.

Once gathered together, try on your business uniform and stand before a full length mirror. To force more objectivity onto the reflection before you, try holding a plain paper or cardboard mask over your face--you'll find your total appearance takes on a new look. If you find yourself asking "Who is that person?" then you're on the way to self-improvement. Color yourself successful so far!

BASIC BUSINESS WARDROBE

Two tailored suits, one in a dark basic color, the other in a light, neutral color.

Two blouses or shirts, one white and tailored, the other in a light color and a bit dressier--striped for men, dressier fabric for women.

Two pairs of shoes, one pair in a dark basic color to go with your dark suit, and the other pair in a neutral medium shade, to wear with your lighter suit.

Outerwear, like a topcoat, lightweight raincoat, umbrella, attache' case and handbag.

Underwear, basic undergarments including hosiery, and cushioned insoles if you'll be on your feet a lot.

"Costly thy habit as thy purse can buy,
But not expressed in fancy;
rich, not gaudy;
For the apparel oft proclaims the man."

--William Shakespeare (1564-1616)

COLOR ANALYSIS

Is a color analysis necessary to look your best? No. Of course not. But it can be informative and bring you some objectivity about your appearance. This applies to both men and women.

What can you expect to learn from a color analysis? First you'll learn what colors and shades of colors make you look your best. Color analysis is based on the three primary colors: red, yellow, and blue, and your skin's reaction to them. With red as a mid-point, you'll be "tested" with colors and shades of colors toward both remaining primary colors, yellow (warm) and blue (cool). Your individual complexion will take on a more appealing, healthy glow from either the yellow side or the blue side, indicating your best color choice will have undertones of that primary color.

You will also learn if your hair color flatters your face as well, and get some suggestions on how to change or enhance it. Women usually get a cosmetic makeover and a lesson in skin care (men should ask about conditioning skin as well). You'll learn what your "power" colors are, and, if the consultant is schooled in wardrobe planning, a sampling of what colors to choose when building your wardrobe. For example, your dark suit might be a royal or navy blue, your light neutral suit a pale gray of a different fabric and style, and your blouse or shirt stark white. With this particular combination, the use of hot pink as an accent color works well—like a hot pink rosebud in the lapel of a blue suit worn over a white blouse or shirt.

If your consultant is also schooled in fabrics, you will learn about textures as well as colors for putting your best face forward.

Rough textured fabrics tend to make your complexion look smoother, while smooth fabrics tend to make your complexion rougher. For example, if you have a rough or scarred or ruddy complexion, pick out textured fabrics for your suits—uneven weaves in coarse or heavy fibers. If you are blessed with a fine, smooth complexion, you can easily wear the smooth fabrics like satin, and appear even finer-of-skin when wearing textured goods.

13

On the other hand, if your body bulges more than you would like to admit, a smooth, satin-type fabric will only emphasize it. Every bulge will be highlighted with the shine of the fabric, drawing attention to that spot. Shiny fabrics reflect light, whereas textured fabrics absorb it.

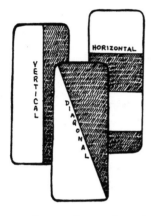

Perhaps your consultant has had some schooling or experience in clothing design, and will advise you to wear vertical lines for a taller, slimmer look. Horizontal lines will give you a shorter, wider look, and diagonal lines can serve to slim you down and stretch you up all at the same time. The three elements of color, texture, and design must go hand in hand to be effective. It's not bad business to seek some professional advice and invest in yourself!

How do you find a good color consultant? You guessed it--more research!

Ask your friends. Judge their results. Check the *Yellow Pages* under "Color Consultants" and make a few phone calls. You can spend anywhere from two hours and $25 to two days and over $200 for color and wardrobe assistance.

You'll want to ask for credentials--where was the consultant trained? Has the consultant studied clothing, textiles, and art? How many years has the consultant been doing color analysis? Wardrobe planning? Is the consultant a licensed cosmetologist (required in some states to apply cosmetics)? What brand of cosmetics will be used? You don't want to get into ones you are allergic to. Will the consultant give references--names and numbers of clients that you can call to ask about the service? And, how long will it take and how much will it cost? What does it include?

When you find a consultant that meets your needs, make an appointment. Plan to take notes while you are there, you may need to refer to them later.

If you choose to bypass the color consultant, you can pick up some good tips from library books on the subject, although I agree with others that color analysis done from a book by an untrained eye can be difficult if not misleading altogether. By all means check out a couple of books on business dressing and wardrobe planning.

VOICE ANALYSIS

Have you ever been really impressed with someone, only to have that impression dashed when he opened his mouth to speak?

Not everyone who is well versed and well dressed is well spoken. You've met them--some whine, some talk too loud and too long, and some still carry the high pitched voice from their "terrible two's." In short, you find them not pleasant to be around, much less buy anything from them. You are not going to join their group.

There are exercises you can do to improve your voice. You'll want to work on tone, clarity, volume, pitch, speed, quantity, and quality. Get out your little tape recorder!

For starters, grab a newspaper or magazine and read some of the ads into your tape recorder. Then play it back, and listen as if a stranger were talking to you. What do you hear? Is the pitch of your voice too high? This can be irritating and less convincing in a sales presentation, and especially over the phone, when the one you are trying to impress thinks you are merely a youngster and therefore not knowledgeable.

Do you enunciate clearly? Can you easily understand every word you say or do you mumble? Do you talk too fast or too slow? It's good to try for a healthy blend of both (more about that in Section 2).

Now read the same ads again into your tape recorder, but this time make a concentrated effort to speak slower and lower. Most of us speak too high-pitched, but if your voice sounded too low for comfortable listening, then raise it some. If you are self conscious or unsure of yourself, you may notice that your voice is so soft that you can't be heard. Turn up the volume! Likewise, if you notice it's very loud, maybe from a habit of yelling at the kids, then soften it a little.

Compare your taped voice with that of a radio announcer or travelogue narrator. You want to be as clearly understood, and working on your enunciation can help achieve that. When you whisper, for example, you are more careful with pronunciation. Your lips take more shape with each sound or syllable, as if you expect to be lip-read. You can notice this more closely yourself by folding your ears forward with your hands and whispering. Whisper into your tape recorder and replay it. Did you understand every word?

Soon you will be giving your sales presentation to all types of people, and some may have hearing impairments, so it is best to pronounce each and every word and number properly to avoid any misunderstanding. It will help to practice on a daily basis, using your tape recorder. Begin by repeating the numbers zero through ten as follows:*

0. Oh 1. Wun 2. Too
3. Th-r-ee 4. Fo-er
5. Fi-iv 6. Siks
7. Sev-en 8. Ate 9. Nien
10. Ten.

It will also help to reiterate the alphabet on a daily basis, not in a contest of speed, but slowly and precisely, rolling the letters around in your mouth and over your lips as if each were a favorite food!

Because you may be asked to give both numbers and letters in the course of selling or writing orders, it is important that you learn the names most commonly used to identify letters of the alphabet. Saying the alphabet letter followed by the

---

* TELEPHONE TECHNIQUES THAT SELL, by Charles Bury

corresponding name avoids confusion, especially over the telephone. Practiced daily, they will soon be committed to memory:

A as in Alice	N as in Nelly
B as in Bertha	O as in Oliver
C as in Charles	P as in Paul
D as in David	Q as in Quaker
E as in Edward	R as in Robert
F as in Frank	S as in Sam
G as in George	T as in Tom
H as in Henry	U as in Utah
I as in Ida	V as in Victor
J as in James	W as in William
K as in Kate	X as in Xray
L as in Louis	Y as in Young
M as in Mary	Z as in Zebra

When you get bored with numbers and letters, try singing one of your favorite songs as you do other work. Remember to include use of your entire vocal instrument when voicing each word--breath, vocal chords, tongue, cheeks, and lips. If you think you need professional coaching, try a few singing lessons or sign up with a teacher of elocution! Consider professional therapy for speech impediments.

Listen to the professionals--radio and television. Notice their enunciation, speed, pitch (high or low), pauses, and enthusiasm. Take note of what you like and incorporate it into your voice; take note of what you don't like and make a point to not do the same!

BODY LANGUAGE

The voice that comes from your lips is not the only language that will impress your customer. Your "body language," the way you move your body--head, eyes, mouth, arms, torso, legs, feet, and hands--all influence the acceptance of your sales presentation.

You want to aim for good posture: sit tall, stand tall, and walk tall. Keep hand and arm gestures fluid in motion and moderate of speed. A quick dash of the arm might frighten an unsuspecting customer, sending any semblance of attention right out the window! Like preparing your speaking voice, you also will practice correct body language.

Begin by observing others, both in real life and on television. Watch their mannerisms--how do they walk, stand, sit? How do they move their arms, eyes? Do they tilt the head? When one news-anchor looks toward the other, do you follow suit? When the spokesperson for a product looks at that product, do you look at it also? That is one of many small but calculated moves--we tend to watch what someone else is watching. Have you ever encountered a crowd looking up at a tall building? Did you automatically look up too?

Always observe, and make a mental note of mannerisms you like and those you don't. Copy accordingly, and bring out the full length mirror!

Some distance away from the mirror, say ten feet or so, place a straight backed chair, facing the mirror. Practice walking to the chair and sitting down, placing your feet, ankles, legs, arms and hands where they look the most respectable. Practice also without the chair, walking toward the mirror until you develop an approach you like. It should be fluid, not rushed but not lagging. For more hints on body language, how to read your customer's and how to use yours to enhance your sales presentation, do some outside reading (see Appendix for suggestions).

Your first contact with a customer will be your greeting. Your "Hello" or "How do you do" will often be coupled with a smile and a handshake. The smile must be friendly and sincere, and the handshake must be firm and confident. Standing to greet someone always shows respect and good manners, and helps get you off to a proper start.

Following the greeting, you might gracefully gesture with your arm and hand where the customer should take place--is a table and chair available? The entire showroom? A door to your office? Once located, you will want to offer coffee, tea, or water, especially if the presentation will be longer than twenty minutes.

Let the customer be seated first, then select a firm chair for yourself rather than sink into a sofa like dirty water swirling down a drain! You need to be at eye level or slightly above your customer, to make eye contact easier during your presentation. Eye contact is very important, but if you need to bring emphasis to the written word, then point directly at it with a pen or pencil and look at it yourself while turning the paper toward the customer. You'll find he follows your lead. (The actual delivery of your presentation will be covered in Section 2. It involves not only the content--what you have to say--but also voice and body language--how you say it--and how to involve the customer--senses.)

Upon close of the presentation, rise from your chair, thank the person for their time, assure that they have all the information needed to make a decision, and shake hands once again while gesturing and escorting them to the exit.

Pleasing body language is something you should practice. Be objective about the way you handle your body, and strive to correct any mannerisms you don't like. With time, it will become habit. You needn't practice walking with a book on your head. In fact, you may be better advised to read a book on posture and body language instead!

ATTITUDE

No matter how gracefully you carry yourself, no matter how impeccably dressed you are, and no matter how perfect a sales presentation you give, if your attitude is rotten--so also are your results!

Respect for yourself and your product must shine through your attitude to your customer. Be cheerful, but not overly so. Be sincere and you'll be taken sincerely. Know your product so well that there is not one question you cannot answer or know where the answer is.

Dress and conduct yourself in a business-like manner not only when giving your sales presentation, but also when working in your office or shop, homebased or otherwise.

Be enthusiastic and positive about your product and business. Think of your encounter with a potential customer as a service—the customer has a problem or a need, and your product will fill it. You know it will, because you know your product and you know yourself. Enthusiasm is contagious. Display it for your product and your customer gets enthused as well. Display indifference, and so will your customer. If you're having a bad day, maybe you should reschedule your appointments?

There are times for all of us when enthusiasm slips away. You begin to wonder if you are pursuing the right course. Do you really want to be in business? Is it worth the struggle? What is the answer?

That is the time to note, on paper, the reasons for and against your ultimate goal. You may find, when all the pros and cons are listed, that the pros outweigh the cons by a good margin. That is the time to reinforce your subconscious with all the positive reasons for continuing your efforts; to visualize the end result: a thriving business that brings happiness and prosperity.

"I never stopped trying...and I never tried stopping."

Dolly Parton, explaining her success in business.

To learn about positive thinking, visualization, and reinforcing your subconscious, read a few books (check the Appendix for suggestions). A positive outlook and visualizing your goals will help you stay on course. There are hundreds, maybe thousands, of books written on the subject, and for good reason: it works! Purchasing a few for regular study might be the smallest price you'll pay towards a successful business, but not all prices are monetary!

A Reflection on Attitude

A good number of my career years were spent working in the office of new car dealerships. It's a great place to work if you want to see all types of salesmen and women. Some are worth studying, to learn for your own future in sales. Others are a bit of comic relief, but not to be emulated for their selling abilities.

One fellow I recall had worked for the same dealership, in sales, for a number of years. Then came a new management team with a new and positive approach to selling and service. Sales meetings were held weekly, training the salesforce in product knowledge, personal habits, and attitude. Well, "Jones" was stuck so deeply in the depths of pessimism he couldn't get out.

I overheard part of his sales presentation one lunch hour. A woman was asking for a certain shade of blue on the model car she had selected.

"Well, now," Jones explained as he walked her past my office, "I'm not too sure we can get that color. It's really tough to get right now. We might not be able to find it for you."

Oh how disappointed she looked, following him into the manager's office. The rest of the conversation I could not hear, but it **should** have gone something like this:

"You've got good taste, Mam! That's a real popular color right now! If we don't have it in stock, we'll locate it for you! When will you want to take delivery?"

I'm not inferring that her color choice <u>was</u> available somewhere, but it's more likely that being positive could have encouraged her into another color, or a different model car in her color, and the sale saved.

Feeling Blue?

Start a "fan mail" file. In this file, keep all letters or notes from clients that praise your goods or services; when verbally complimented, make a note of it and put into your file.

On a "bad day," scan through the notes, reinforcing your attitude that you do indeed have a good product or service to sell.

The facts don't lie!

PAYING YOUR DUES

Aside from financial outlay or investment, there are other costs to pay when building a business. It is endearingly known as "paying your dues."

One way you begin to pay dues is by giving up things that filled your leisure hours in order to work on your business. For example, you might have to give up a favorite television show in order to have time to research and write your sales presentation. You might have to give up shopping or lunching with friends to make your phone calls and set appointments. You may have to give up Saturday morning golf to shop the sales for office furniture or scout the competition. Giving-up is part of the price you willingly pay to begin your business. The alternative is to postpone.

Go ahead and enjoy your favorite shows, your shopping, your lunches, and your golf. After all, you can always start next month.

Imagine next month is January. It is too soon after the holidays, so you can't start then. In February there are holidays—the Presidents' Birthdays and Valentine's Day.

March of course is St.Patrick's Day, so you can't do much that month.

April brings income tax to figure, or perhaps you'll be tied up with Easter preparations.

May would be the month to start, but you must make plans for Mothers Day and Memorial Day. So how about June?

The kids get out of school in June. You're planning for vacation, not to mention Fathers Day and maybe a class reunion.

July is out of the question! Big parade and fireworks show and picnic on the fourth; friends are coming from out of town. You'll be too busy!

August would be a good month to start... No! You must get the kids ready for school next month, or take that vacation postponed in June; or paint the house; or visit your sister in Philadelphia.

September starts with the Labor Day weekend. Then the kids must be sent off to school, and you've got to get those storm windows back up.

October will be it. There's only Columbus Day (you don't celebrate that), and how long can it take to sew up a couple of Halloween costumes?

November is here before you know it. Gutters to clean, Thanksgiving dinner plans to make, holiday decorations to find....

December brings cards to write and mail, gifts to purchase and wrap and ship, parties to plan, decorations to hang, and make reservations for New Year's Eve! You'll start your business next month!

How do you find time to "pay your dues?" You get tough. You set goals. You establish a place and a time for work. And you don't tolerate interruptions!

 You give up your favorite television program. You organize your duties around the home and pass some of them on to spouse or children--it is their share of the dues. You become more efficient and so does your family! You may have to stay up later at night doing research, or rise an hour earlier in the morning, when you can have time to yourself.

> *"If you have a job without aggravations, you don't have a job. "*
> *Malcolm Forbes*

It is imperative that you have your own little room or corner or shop in which to close the door and do your work. You may have to remind the kids or friends who interrupt you that you are "working right now," and can help or visit with them later. This is especially difficult with a homebased business.

Children will need to be trained; they will need projects of their own lined up and must understand that although this is a new experience, you <u>must not</u> <u>be</u> <u>disturbed</u> (unless someone is dying or the building is on fire!).

Do not expect total cooperation the first day. One of your "payments" will be training the intruders and reinforcing your commitment to work. Friends who call to chat, and they will, will have to be politely reminded that these are your working hours now, but you'll be anxious to return the call in the evening. (Your really true friends will understand and help you; the ones who get upset are jealous—let them simmer for awhile.)

When you have collected your work space and your wits, what do you do first? You pencil out a business plan; a road map that will take you from where you are now to where you want to be. You set goals.

GOAL SETTING

"If you set nothing for a goal, you'll surely attain it." I don't know who said that, but it's painfully true.

When finding and keeping customers, you'll want to set goals—a timetable for accomplishments—to keep yourself moving along in the right direction. Depending on where you are in your business-building, your goals might start with (1) researching your product, (2) preparing yourself and your wardrobe, (3) writing your sales presentation, (4) perfecting your sales presentation for delivery, (5) researching potential customers (also called prospecting), and (6) making appointments.

From these six goals you will progress to keeping appointments, making follow up calls, and developing a system for continually increasing your business base (number of customers).

If you are manufacturing and selling your own product, you will have manufacturing goals or deadlines entered on your goal sheet as well.

Setting goals is like preparing a nine-course dinner: you plan ahead of time what you are serving, how long the preparation takes, and at what time each dish must be started to be ready for serving at its peak flavor and appearance. You plan also the setting—the tableware, the linens, crystal, flowers, music, seating arrangement, and all the tiny details that make it a success.

So also must you plan your business—all the tiny details that will lead you to success!

All you need to make your Goal Sheet is some

1. do research

2. get color analysis & makeover

3. coordinate wardrobe

4. write presentation

5. make appointments

paper (several pieces please, as goal sheets rarely begin in organized fashion), a pencil, and a twelve month calendar.

Label the top of a page "Goal Sheet." Then list, somewhere in an upper corner, these three words: 1. Specific, 2. Attainable, 3. Organized. These are the three Nitty-Gritty-Rules (NGR) of a workable goal sheet!

Next begin to list your goals, just as they pop into your mind and in no particular order. Your first might be "to have a successful business," a classic, reasonable goal. Continue writing down your goals, which will include your preparation of product knowledge and personal knowledge, writing your sales presentation, finding customers, making appointments, placing advertisements, buying a new suit, and so on. Like the nine-course dinner, make an effort to think of all the tiny details that come into play before you reach success.

When you have exhausted your supply of goals, return to the top and consider each goal in terms of NGR#1 (Nitty-Gritty-Rule #1). Specific.

Goals must be specific. In terms of having a "successful business" you probably mean monetary gain. Money. Is your goal simply "Money"? No, you must be specific again--how much money? And within what period of time? Per month? Per year? Write it down! Now you have something specific.

Proceed to NGR#2--attainable. Goals must be attainable. Set them in small amounts or steps, never so high that you can't reach them as planned or you may become dejected and give up altogether.

For example, if you're setting a goal for telephone work, instead of aiming for $500 in sales, try only for making an appointment to show your goods, or to leave a sample and literature. Make it your "break-the-ice" goal; the sale will come later. If you are in retail or have appointments booked to give your sales presentation, set a modest dollar or unit amount to reach, then work on raising that amount over a period of months and years. (See MONEY, MATHEMATICS & GOALS later in this section).

If your goal is product research, consider realistically how much time you'll need to spend at sales meetings, at the library, and product testing at home before giving yourself a deadline. The same goes for personal improvement, creating a workspace, finding customers, and the rest.

After you have modified your goals to attainable heights, then is the time for NGR#3--organize.

Rearrange the goals in the order they must be completed; first things first. Carefully consider the time needed to complete each one and, counting on your calendar, write next to each goal the date or deadline you give yourself to have it done! Also write it on your calendar!

Rewrite your Goal Sheet if you prefer a neater list, and post it where you can check your progress daily. If you have three areas in which to research your product and have allowed yourself three weeks to have it done, then you must complete one per week to be on schedule. If you start slipping behind, give up another leisure activity to stay on target.

To help you stay motivated, put up little signs around your workspace like "YOU CAN DO IT!" or "STAY ON TARGET!" or "PAY DUES TODAY, PAY ME TOMORROW!" My personal contribution is the sign that simply reads "G G G" (Get up, Get dressed, and Get going!)

One multi-level-marketing group I visited for a few meetings promoted the idea of making "Dream Boards." Each member was to paste, onto a large posterboard, pictures cut from magazines and such of things that they wanted to eventually acquire. Things like money, a new car, a new home, vacation trips, jewelry, college for the kids, new golf clubs, a grand piano, and so on. This "Dream Board" was to be placed in the bedroom where nobody else could see it, and by studying it daily for  a few minutes, the desires for these things would become ingrained into the subconscious mind. Then, putting the action in place to reach these dreams (goals), the subconscious mind would eventually fulfill them. That was the plan.

Did it work? Not for me--I never did mine! But I can tell you that some years later my husband and I pictured, mentally, that we would sell our truck and camper and somehow, we knew not how, we would get a Jeep and a small motorhome. We didn't make a Dream Board, but we did visualize it, day after day, and finally put an ad in the paper.

The very next day our truck and camper sold to the first person who came to see it, and for the exact price we were asking! After some months of shopping, we found our Jeep.

Well, that worked so well, we tried the same attitude on a building lot located in a somewhat depressed area. We had tried three times before to sell it. "Why not try it again?" we questioned. "Maybe we could get enough to buy a small motorhome." So we listed it again, but this time we pictured it sold. You guessed it—it sold! And we found our motorhome.

Does it work? I won't guarantee it, but I'm starting a Dream Board now! My first entry is a drawing of a piggy bank with $500,000 inside it!

MONEY, MATHEMATICS, & GOALS

$500,000 is a nice round figure for a piggy bank, but is rarely the total sales for a small business in its first year. But yearly sales is the yardstick by which business success is measured.

This book will not delve into accounting and all its variables (get a CPA), but you do need to know a little math in order to set reasonable goals. Time for paper, pencil, a calculator, and maybe a calendar.

For a reasonable yearly sales figure, simply estimate what you can sell in one week and multiply that by the number of weeks in a year (52). Or estimate what you can sell per month and multiply by twelve.

To set goals, however, you will probably want to work with the amount of money you need to make as income or wages. To calculate that, you will need to know your percentage of commission or net profit. That is, what percent of sales can you "take home?"

Let's say you need an income of $200 per week, and you know that your rate of commission or net profit is 10% of sales. If $200 is 10%, then divide the $200 by 10 to find one percent, and multiply that by 100 to get 100%, or the total amount of sales you'll need ($2000).

From there you can set more specific goals. Assuming you need to sell $2,000 per week and you only work five days per week, then you need to sell an average of $400 per day to meet your goal. ($2,000 divided by five days). Knowing this, you can check daily to see if you are "on target" for your goal.

Use your calendar for setting nonfinancial goals as well. Suppose you want to mail promotional flyers to prospective customers. First you'll set a goal date for mailing. Then backup on your calendar, maybe three days to allow for folding, addressing, and printing delays. That will be your goal date for picking up the flyers from the printer.

Two days or so before that might be your goal date for getting the material to the printer. And, allowing yourself a week to ten days for gathering information, writing, and pasteup of your mechanical, you come back even closer to the present to set your goal date for beginning the flyer.*

When each goal date is met as planned, your flyer is completed and mailed out on time! A pat on the back for you!

Thus far you've been told how to research for product knowledge, give up your leisure time, set your goals, dream your dreams, improve your attitude, your posture, your wardrobe, your handshake, your voice, your complexion, and your speech. You should be about "up to your ears" by now!

THE EARS HAVE IT!

Let's assume that you can hear, but do you know how to listen? One of the best sales tools you can posses is an attentive ear. Listen. Hear what your customer wants. "Find a need and fill it."

---

* for more information on making your own newsletters, brochures, and flyers, see HOW TO MAKE NEWSLETTERS, BROCHURES & OTHER GOOD STUFF without a computer system. By H.Gregory

Practice listening to friends and acquaintances. What are they really saying? What are their needs? Question, don't assume. The salesperson who does all the talking and no listening is missing the point. And the sale. And the referrals and the repeat business.

Learn to listen; give your complete attention, keep eye contact stable, and when the need has been expressed to you, repeat it for confirmation. You must understand the problem correctly before offering a solution (your product).

And now, having improved your hearing along with everything else, you're ready to retrieve that product-research and start preparing your sales presentation! GO FOR IT!

WRITING THE SALES PRESENTATION

What is a sales presentation? It's something you have been doing all your life! As a child, you sold your mother on the idea to buy you a candy bar or toy at the market. As a teenager, you sold your folks on letting you go on an outing away from home, or borrowing the family car for an evening, or breaking curfew. As an adult, you persuaded your  employer into giving you a raise in pay, or convinced your spouse of marriage or a major household purchase. You sold a concept, an idea. It is the same in business.

You'll need to write a sales presentation, and that can be easily done in several small steps. Focus upon each step completed as one small success, until finally the entire project is finished. It's a little like following a recipe--you assemble all the ingredients, measure carefully, and follow instructions. Before you know it, your project is done and ready to serve!

The first step in writing your sales presentation is to gather all your product information and research notes together with some pencils and a supply of paper. Sort the information into two groups: (1) benefits, or points of value to the customer, and (2) limits, or possible objections or drawbacks to the customer.

Of the benefits, single out three or four you consider to be major or most important. Before transforming them into your sales presentation, you should know the basics of the plan.

You begin with a rough draft, never a finished presentation. Your goal is to write about 500 words total—enough to fill a double spaced typewritten page on both sides.

First comes the introduction: who and what you are. You'll introduce yourself and your product. This should last two minutes only.

Next will be the body of your presentation. Here you give the benefits, the whys and wherefores, and will take about six or seven minutes to deliver. You'll include in the body all the information the customer will need: what the product is, sizes, colors, service included, prices, savings, financing options, return policies, and etc.

The close or call-to-action is the last part of your presentation as planned. It is the most important part, creating motivation and urgency to buy your product, and may last up to fifteen minutes. The close or call-to-action is point where you ask the customer for an order.

During your presentation, you will encounter objections. These are not planned in your sales presentation, but because you have researched your product thoroughly, you will be prepared with answers. Handling objections is covered in more detail later in this section.

Because you are well-informed and well-experienced about your product, interruptions will not shove you off course. You will be flexible enough within your planned sales presentation to handle the interruption and resume your presentation. This will happen whether you give your presentation in person in your store, in the customer's home or yours, or by telephone. You still begin it all with the introduction.

Start with six pieces of blank paper. Label the first one "Introduction," the second "Benefit #1," the third "Benefit #2," the fourth "Benefit #3," the fifth "Benefit #4," and the sixth "Close" or "Call to Action." What you will be noting on these six papers at first are reminders for each subject or category.

On the "Introduction" paper, make note of things like your name, your product, that it can be a good point to name-drop, if possible, and also a good time to use "ice breaker" comments, like a small compliment on the person's home, jewelry, clothes, or kids.

The papers for "Benefit #1" (and #2,#3,#4) comprise the body of your presentation. Benefit #1 should be the most important one, the one of most value, i.e., money-saving, time-saving, health-giving, etc. List the four benefits you have selected, one to a page, in order of their importance. Then return to Benefit #1 and note in words and phrases what makes it a value. Why should the customer want to buy it? How will it help him/her? Does it have a contribution to society as a whole—ecology? energy? What sizes, colors, price, availability? What is the guarantee? Continue on through Benefits #2, #3, and #4, noting on each one the particular value and reasons a customer would want to buy your product.

On your "Close" or "Call to Action" page, you'll want to remind yourself to put the customer into the "Yes Mode" by covering a series of small points to which the customer agrees. You'll need to create an urgency or motivation to buy, counter objections, and ask for the sale. Small points to close on might be color—would they prefer green or white?—size, delivery date approval—would Monday or Wednesday be good for delivery?—how many of the item, how will they pay for it—cash, check, or credit card—all answered while you complete the sales order form.

Also on your "Close" sheet, you'll want to remind yourself to thank the customer for her time. A person's time is very important. Once given, it can never be replaced. It is a most precious commodity.

Having noted all this basic information on your worksheets, return again to the "Introduction," to begin writing your sales presentation.

Imagine that you are speaking to a potential customer. What would you say that contains your introduction information? Try several different approaches, like "Hello, my name is Mary Jones," or "Good morning, Mrs. Ringfinger? My name is Mary Jones and I'm calling about XYZ Company's furniture sale." Write down the approach that sounds the best and most comfortable to you. Don't worry about your grammar, just write like you talk--friendly, informative, and sincere. Avoid being dogmatic although your purpose is to inform.

Also in your introduction, you might explain briefly why you are qualified to sell the product. No bragging, please! Give the customer some background on yourself: your schooling, special training, work experience, awards, etc., but move right along to the body of your presentation.

Benefits #1, #2, #3, and #4 make up the body of your presentation. As you did with the introduction, imagine that you are telling a friend of this wonderful product or service, including all the values and information listed on Benefit page #1. Write down the wording just as you imagined it. Then do the same for the pages on Benefit #2, #3, and #4.

Your aim here is to be precise and concise, giving exact information (sizes, colors, prices, etc.), in the fewest words possible. Here it will help to sell your product or service in terms of a philosophy or idea or concept. Share your conviction in your product as you would share news of a new and wonderful restaurant in town!

Why do you believe in the product? What has it done for you? For other customers? Maybe your product saves money, or time, or energy, or the environment. Or maybe it just makes you feel good! Share that with your customer. Use words that create vision, or feelings. Compare the benefit to a familiar, comfortable object or idea--something your customer can relate to on a pleasant basis.

When you are sharing a conviction or philosophy

EXAMPLE: ACTUAL SALES PRESENTATION

Candice Powder manufactures beach cover ups, and is marketing them to women's apparel and swim suit shops. She has made appointments by phone to show her product.

This is how her appointment went with the owner of a women's apparel shop:

Candice: "Good morning, Ms. Owner? I'm Candice Powder from Candy's Coverups. We had an 11:00 o'clock appointment?!

Ms. Owner: "Oh yes, please come in!"

Candice: "Would you prefer to see these in your office?"

Ms. Owner: "Yes, right this way."

(Candice notices Ms. Owner is wearing blue, so removes a blue coverup from her sample case and hands it to her. Ms. Owner begins to examine it.)

Candice: "Each coverup comes with its own matching, plastic lined, zippered case-- for carrying your wet suit home from the pool!"

Ms. Owner: "Un huh. That's good! What sizes do you have?"

Candice: "One size fits all--basically from Missy 10 thru 20. I see you do sell larger sizes here."

Ms. Owner: "Yes, that's why I asked. What other colors do you have?"

Candice:	"Here's some samples of the colors. We've got white, peach, aqua, and the blue you are holding now. They're all 100% pima cotton--notice how soft and comfortable they are?"
Ms. Owner:	"Yes. They are nice. How much are they?"
Candice:	"Retail is $32. They're only $12 each OR you can order six assorted colors for $55 total--a profit of $137.00!"
Ms. Owner:	"OK. I'll take six. How soon can you have them here?"
Candice:	"I have two in the car you can have today--would one peach and one blue be OK?"
Ms. Owner:	"Yes, that'll be fine."
Candice:	"Good. I'll get those two, and the rest will be shipped within the week."
	(Candice rushes to her car, brings back the two coverups and writes up the order. She thanks Ms. Owner, gathers her papers and samples and exits quickly.)
Candice:	"Thank you, Ms. Owner. I'll be calling you in a week or so to make sure everything is OK."
Ms. Owner:	"Yes. Fine. Thank you."

Once in her car, Candice notes the transaction on her 3x5 follow up card, and will call in a week to make sure delivery was satisfactory.

with someone, rather than merely selling a product, it becomes easier to develop a logical sequence of benefits. Think of it as a little "story" about your product, and that story will help you get back on track when interrupted during your presentation.

You'll want to motivate the customer to buy during your "Close." One way is to show the customer that she needs your product. Create a need and fill it. It's a good idea to have available not only the product, but also newspaper and magazine articles promoting it or its benefits. These articles should NOT be written by your manufacturer, nor advertising for the product, but objective opinions of others in the field. Endorsement by an unrelated source will give credibility to your presentation.

Imagine again, sharing your enthusiasm with a friend, urging them to try the product for the benefits it gives. Write down that imaginary conversation, just as you shared it with your friend.

You'll know you're into the "Close" of your presentation when the customer begins making objections or asking questions. Don't continue as planned. Stop and handle each question or objection (which is really a form of question, or request for more information). After each objection has been met, you ask for the sale. Not hard-sell, like "shall we write up the order for the car now?" but rather point by point, as you complete the sales form. What color would you like? Would you want the leather upholstery or the fabric? Fabric is a good choice, it's very comfortable in the summer! You would like air conditioning in the car, wouldn't you? And the sale goes on. Don't shy away from objections!

The last worksheet you'll want to make is one labeled "Objections." Using the research papers you made on objections or limits to your product, list any and all objections you can think of that the customer may present to you. Objections can be about the product or service itself, your background or qualifications, financing, or lack of time. How do you handle them?

Sample Dialogue: Objection

Scene: Mrs. Wall has nearly sold a ten pound box of Scrubsoap on its merits of non-pollution and economy.

Customer: *"I think it's too heavy for me to handle."*

Mrs. Wall: *"Yes, Mrs. Ceiling, the Scrubsoap box is heavy. It's loaded with cleaning power, rather than lightweight fillers that can clog your machine! I'm sure you see the value in that, don't you?"*

Customer: *"I've used Lyesoap for years honey, and I've never had any clogs in my machine!"*

Mrs. Wall: *"Of course you haven't! But they can build up very slowly, you know, over a period of years. Then one day it's enough to clog your machine! That calls for repairs or a new machine! Scrubsoap can remove those clogs with repeated washings.*

"How about trying it for three months and, if you don't like it, I'll buy it back from you?"

(Mrs. Wall makes the sale)

HANDLING OBJECTIONS

First, you agree. Then you turn it around to a positive aspect. You'll find that customers "don't like, don't need, can't afford, will consider it later," or "don't have the time." Your job is to find out the real objection and satisfy it.

Maybe they need to ask someone else before purchasing, maybe you haven't given your presentation clearly or didn't qualify your customer beforehand (see QUALIFYING YOUR CUSTOMER in Section 2).

The basic formula for handling objections is to (1) agree, then (2) offer a solution in terms of a benefit or, (3) ask if there are any other objections. This will often get you away from one you can't handle and on to one you can.

You might want to do more research and preparation for handling objections. Start by watching how others handle yours—did you like it? Did it work? Visit your competition. Ask and object. Make note of what you liked and store that tactic in your memory.

In my days working for automobile dealerships, it was a common practice for salesmen and women, and often a male and female posing as a married couple, to "shop" the competition. This gave them insight into sales—indeed an advantage to those just learning, as their work shift was usually scheduled for the non-prime time. Prime time, the time when most buyers are out, is given first to the senior sales department, the "pros" of the business. Although trainees lost the advantage of selling during prime time, they gained the advantage of scouting the competition at a time when their "pros" were on duty!

They learned quickly that to agree with an objection doesn't mean to agree with the objection, but to agree that there is an objection. From there you question for more information, attempting to find out the real objection.

Your response might go something like this: your customer doesn't like the color. You agree by saying, "I understand. Is it all blues you don't like or just this shade?" Now you will get some specific information to work with. If the answer is "all blues," present other color choices to the customer, asking "which color do you like the best?" Remember, you are trying to determine what the customer wants and needs, so you can supply it!

With the color choice made, you are one point closer to closing the sale! The next might be style, size, accessories, and so on--sold point by point until the sale is made.

PRACTICE! PRACTICE! PRACTICE!

When your sales presentation is finally written, you'll want to practice giving it over and over again until it's ingrained in your memory and no longer sounds labored or memorized. You want it to be natural, to know the content and sequence or story so well that no interruption can throw you off course.

Start by using your tape recorder. Record and listen, and listen, and listen. Then record again, changing what you didn't like, and listen some more. Let it play while you do other chores, or while you're driving in the car. Change what you don't like--wording, comparisons, voice tone and pitch, speed, and pronunciation.

Continue your practice by using your full length mirror again. Position your chair, walk to it, seat yourself gracefully, and give your sales presentation to that person in the mirror. Change what body movements you don't like, and practice eye contact--whether directly with the customer, or bringing attention to the product or literature.

After the sessions with your tape recorder and mirror, you might like to try it out on a friend. Pick a supportive friend, one who will prod you with unplanned objections and questions. One who will tell you what isn't comfortable to hear or see, and will make suggestions for improvement along with giving you praise when you're good!

Keep practicing until you're ready to meet your first real customer!

SUMMARY

1. Research your product. Test it yourself; gather literature from supplier, manufacturer, sales leader; attend meetings; visit the competition; visit the Public Library; study on a regular basis, and takes notes.

2. Develop a good self-image; work on your personal appearance, body language, quality of voice, and positive attitude.

3. Start paying your dues; sacrifice leisure time activities to make time for preparation; set goals that are specific, attainable, and organized; learn to listen to what your customer is really saying.

4. Prepare your sales presentation, beginning with the introduction, then the body, and on to the close or sale. Practice handling objections by first agreeing that there is one, then offering a solution to it or asking for other objections.

5. Practice giving your presentation, into a tape recorder, in front of the mirror, and finally to a dear friend. Keep practicing and improving while you work your way through Section 2:FINDING CUSTOMERS.

SECTION TWO: FIND!

Identifying your customer

Finding your customer

Qualifying your customer

Drop-in customers

Making appointments

Making the call

Giving the sales presentation

The do's & don't's of presentation

Summary

Finding customers is like planting a fine flower garden. First you do the groundwork, cultivating and enriching the soil to its full potential.

Then you select the very best seeds, plant carefully in prearranged locations, water, and wait for them to sprout. When they do, you continue to water and feed them until the plants are strong and tall and bursting with blooms.

Some sprout new buds, flaunting flower after flower for your enjoyment, while others busy themselves making next year's seeds. The garden is an everchanging, exciting renewal of life.

But, occasionally, you have to pull a weed.

IDENTIFYING YOUR CUSTOMER

Before you can plant your concept into a customer's mind, before you can nurture and motivate the sale, before you can assemble your bouquet of buyers, you must know who they are.

To find that out, ask yourself these questions: Who needs my product? Would it be individuals or firms? What age group would they be? Where would they live? Where would they shop? What income level must they have to buy my product? Will they be male or female or both? Children or adults? What profession? What newspapers and magazines do they read? What radio station do they listen to? What television programs do they watch?

By answering such questions, you can develop a list of customer types that are more likely to want your product than those picked at random. The list will help you to find your customers just like knowing what flowers you want in your garden will help you locate the correct seed.

Imagine anyone and everyone who could use your product or service. For example, if you're selling laundry soap: who gets dirty? Who more than others? Maybe they should come first. Little baseball players get dirty; their uniforms must be washed; hospitals must launder sheets or send them to someone who does; hairdressers have lots of towels to wash. The list goes on and on.

FINDING YOUR CUSTOMER

Once you have an idea in mind of just who your customer is--what requirements he must meet to be a likely candidate--you can begin to find him. There are as many ways to look as there are creative ideas in your mind. It is a matter of numbers: the more contacts you make, the more eventual sales you will have. But your chances are increased by "targeting" those contacts.

It's been said that for every three phone calls, you'll make one appointment to give your presentation. And for every three presentations, you'll make one sale! Sometimes you only plant seeds, little ideas that germinate and sprout and finally grow into a new customer. To get your creativity flowing, read through the following list of ideas for finding customers. Which ones can you use? Can others be adapted to your needs?

1. Family and friends. Let them know what you are attempting. Ask for referrals or leads (names of potential customers), but keep in mind that it is often more difficult to sell to those we know than to sell to complete strangers.

2. Referrals. Ask for them as each sales presentation or sale. Ask for them in your follow up work (Section 3).

3. Leads. Names you find or buy. Many communities have organizations that welcome new residents, and will give them your sample or information. You get the name and address for a small fee.

4. Direct mail. Mailing lists can be rented for a specific consumer base, like for computer users, doctors, business executives, apparel shop owners, and etc. You'd be well advised to check out a good book on direct mail before jumping into the expense of it. Direct mail can be used on a smaller scale, however, by sending brochures to family and friends, or including one with each bill you pay!

5. The Public Library. Use directories of organizations, associations, reverse street directories (names and addresses in specific neighborhoods, and often give employment and income date). There are directories on companies as well, giving location, financial condition, and number of employees. Ask the librarian for help.

6. Telephone books. The *Yellow Pages* come in handy if you are targeting types of businesses, like for a mailing or telephone campaign to gift shops, apparel shops, etc. Libraries will have out-of-town and out-of-state telephone directories as well.

7. Garage or Yard sales. Have flyers available during your sale; display a sample of the product; offer a sign-up sheet for those interested.

8. Public places. When visiting public places, such as the supermarket or laudromat, be on guard for remarks that indicate someone might need your product. I have seen approaches made in parking lots, using a quick remark and the slip of a business card. Although I don't advocate soliciting inside a place of business (you're not paying the rent), do keep a supply of business cards with you.

9. Community bulletin boards. Post a flyer showing your product, its benefits, and your phone number. Be cautioned about leaving your phone number and residence address together if you have a homebased business.

10. Newspaper articles. Scan the newspapers daily for likely subjects. In addition to articles about people, there are lists of marriages, divorces, deaths, and births. Sometimes the classified ads will offer prospects--for sale by owner.

11. Public records. On both local and state levels, you'll find lists that might apply. Auto license records, RV ownership, home ownership, motorcycle owners, and small businesses.

12. Trade magazines. Check the *Literary Market Place* in the library for names and addresses. Select a few that apply to your business or customer type and write to them for a "media kit." You'll receive a packet including advertising rates, a sample copy, and readership demographics. Send press releases to the ones that relate to your business. Invite readers to inquire for more information.

13. In-Store promotions. Plan an in-store promotion and invite the public via press release. These promotions are to present your product to the customer while giving away something of value, usually information. You goal will be to gather names and addresses of interested people for your mailing list and to get them into the habit of walking into your store. Sales will come later.

14. Advertising. Newspaper and magazine advertising is relatively expensive for a small business. Magazines have a lead time of two to three months or more, which is not timely for a small business. Read the Small Business Administration's pamphlet on advertising. If you do choose media advertising, remember you must "hit 'em on the head. HARD!" It is a matter of numbers: invite many with your value and few if any will come. You might do better to read the ads that are there for possible leads, or use direct mail to a targeted group.

15. Teach a class or give a workshop in your product area of expertise. Your goal is to get names and addresses of who are interested. You might even charge a small fee for the class!

16. Publish a booklet on your subject area. Sell it in your shop or mail order for a couple of dollars and get names and address of interested people in return. These are leads you generate yourself.

17. Involve employees. They each know an average of 250 people each* and they know your product and your business credibility. Ask for referrals.

18. Start a club. Hold monthly meetings, send newsletters, give member discounts. Attract more members (customers) through members.

19. Hold contests. Get free publicity through press releases and posters. Have a sign up sheet and drawing to generate more leads.

20. Door to door. Cold calling. It's tough, but works for some. Leave samples and information, call back for appointment in five days.

21. Flyers and brochures. Carry them with you always. Get permission to leave on automobiles (violation of law in some places). I've seen them left in public restrooms, auto shop waiting rooms, laundromats, and anywhere people sit and wait for something--usually wanting something to read!

22. Business cards. Hand one out to everyone you meet. Plant seeds. Let them know you are looking for business. You'll be surprised where it will lead: maybe the person you least expect to respond will send you a very good customer!

23. Press releases. Send them regularly for any newsworthy item about your business: when you start, when additional lines are added, when you win

---

*HOW TO SELL ANYTHING TO ANYBODY by Joe Girard

an award or offer a workshop or class, when you hire someone new, etc.

24. Association rosters. Locate trade association member lists at the library and contact members.

25. Share lists. Trade customer names and addresses with a compatible business and mail flyers.

26. Join a group. Community project groups or classes will put you in contact with your neighbors, who will be interested to learn of your business. Let them know you accept referrals.

27. Volunteer work. Sign up for a few hours of volunteer work. Don't worry about making contacts, just enjoy the release from your everyday pace and the benefits of doing for others.

28. Eat out. Can that help? You bet! It's amazing what conversations with the person sitting next to you will lead to. Sit at the counter; carry business cards in your pocket. You needn't eat, even a cup of coffee here and there will bring new leads.

29. Write a column. Either a regular column or article submitted on spec can bring leads. Let the paper know that instead of payment, you'll take a blurb about your business and location at the end of the article.

30. Be flexible. Learn to "roll with the punches," listen to new ideas, and learn to spot opportunity when it knocks on your door.

Always, always be on guard for possible customers or referrals, but be sure each meets your requirements before investing a lot of your valuable time. Be persistent in your determination to build a business.

Jeffrey Lant, publisher of *Jeffrey Lant's Sure-Fire Business Success Catalog*, gives a few business-building tips in an interview-article in *In Business* magazine (October, 1988):

"Use customer testimonials; quote your customers;

put it in the window with an instant picture...."

"Review Chase's Calendar of Events in the library; every kind of offbeat and major event is listed. Find a day or week related to your product...send news releases to newspapers and trade publications 90 days in advance."

You should send for Jeffery Lant's catalog. It lists a lot of books on business building. (Check Appendix for address).

© GREGORY 1988

QUALIFYING YOUR CUSTOMER

What does it mean to "qualify" a customer? It means determining if (1) the customer needs your product, if (2) the customer can afford your product or can be successfully financed, and if (3) the customer is serious about purchasing.

In some businesses it is more critical to qualify customers. For example, a real estate salesperson must verify that the customer is not only serious, but has the income to qualify for a mortgage. If qualification is not done, the salesperson may spend precious hours trying to accomplish a sale that never can be made. It is time wasted for both parties.

Qualifying should be done at the time an appointment is made for giving the sales presentation. The investigation must be subtle; questions must be phrased in the guise of human interest.

To find out if the need is genuine, you might inquire if your type of product has been used before. Yes? Good. No? Why the interest at this time?

To determine income is a delicate matter. You

51

can casually inquire about employment—do you work here in town? How interesting! How long have you been there...maybe you know my cousin Barkley? Oh, you just started! Well, did you retire from your previous job, then?

If financing is likely for the purchase of your product, you know that the customer employed for less than one year will be more difficult to get approved. You must determine a previous length of employment or access to other financing like a credit union.

A sincere interest can bring out the information you need in bits and pieces of everyday conversation. Ask for more detailed information, if needed, during the close of your sale.

DROP-IN CUSTOMERS

If you are a store owner, retail or wholesale, your customers consist largely of "drop-ins." You have no warning, no time to prepare your sales presentation. You don't know if your drop-in is qualified or not, so you must be ready at all times—first with your qualifying inquiry, then with your sales presentation. Your advantage is that drop-ins are interested customers or they wouldn't enter the store!

A smaller number of your customers will telephone you first. That telephone contact is what will or will not bring them to your business. The information in the following subject area can and should be adapted to your needs. Although you may attract adequate business from advertising and referrals, don't discount altogether using a telephone campaign to build new customers.

Rather than making an appointment, your goal will be to let potential customers know you exist, to determine their need for your product, and to invite them to visit your store.

If your time is too limited to make the calls, consider hiring an articulate, intelligent, energetic high school or college student for a few hours per week to identify customers and make the calls.

You might be surprised at the results!

Example: Telephone-Campaign Call

Scene: Mary Mozzerella owns a women's apparel shop, specializing in large sizes. Sales have been down; she needs to find customers without spending heavily on advertising. A telephone campaign is selected: she'll call names from the area directory (random calling).

Mary: *"Hello, Mrs. Budvase?"*
Customer: *"Yes."*
Mary: *"I'm Mary Mozzerella. I'm looking for women in the area who wear large size apparel. Do you fit that category?"*
Customer: *"Heavens, no! I'm the same size seven I was twenty years ago!"*
Mary: *"Oh, lucky you! Would you happen to know of any woman in the area who does wear larger sizes?"*
Customer: *"Well, yes. My friend Dot."*
Mary: *"I'd like very much to invite her to an open house at my shop. Could you give me her name and address?"*

Mrs. Budvase gives Mary the name and address. Not only does Mary have a good prospect, but can use Mrs. Budvase's name when making contact. She thanks Mrs. Budvase and waits for her to hang up first.

MAKING APPOINTMENTS

Though one or two appointments may come about from face-to-face meetings, most of your appointments will be made by telephone. To encourage a successful session, you'll want to first develop a plan. That plan will start with finding a comfortable spot to work. Next will be some goal setting, then preparation of a mini-sales presentation, the making of a Call Sheet, and finally making the calls.

A comfortable setting will not be the livingroom sofa. It will be a room to yourself. One with a desk, telephone, supportive chair, papers, pencils, a calendar, and no interruptions.

In this room you will sit at your desk and decide what to accomplish in a given day: you'll set goals. These will include objectives like how many calls you'll make, how long you will work, whether you'll make the appointment or merely get past the secretary or call-screener to the decision maker (or find out who that is.)

If you have gathered a sizeable list of customers to call, don't plan to get them all called in one day. That's too high a goal, and may discourage you. Try calling three or four per hour to start.

Another goal will be to write two mini-presentations: one for making appointments, and another for answering machines, as you're sure to encounter one! The answering machine message is simple. You have two choices: (1) to hang up without leaving a message, or (2) to state your name (no return telephone number) and that you'll try again. Do not leave your name, your purpose, your number, and expect a return call! You will not get it! And may be quickly put off when you try again!

Leaving just your name and that you'll try again, however, can open a small door. When you call again and reach the customer, your name will have a familiar ring to it and the customer will be curious about what you wanted!

There are two types of appointments you can make. One is to share product information (sales presentation) and the other is to simply leave samples or information, then contact in five days to arrange a time for your sales presentation. You'll start by trying for the sales presentation appointment, but

stay flexible--you might have to make the sample/information kind instead. Whichever you make, consider yourself successful!

Before starting work on your mini-sales presentation, make a list of goals that you want to accomplish that day. For example, your first goal might be to organize your collection of customer names and numbers with the most-likely-to-respond on top. Then you might want to decide how many you will try to reach that day. Next you will want to draft your mini-presentation and practice it a few times, then make your "Call Sheet." Your final goal of the day will be making the calls!

The mini-sales presentation is much like your regular sales presentation. It begins with an introduction, followed by the body, and on to the close. The big difference is this one sells the idea of making an appointment, rather than selling the benefits of the product. And it's much shorter!

You must identify yourself and your product within the first thirty seconds of a telephone sales call. (Check with your local telephone company to find out about regulations on sales calls in your area).

The body sells benefits or values to the customer, but this time they relate to appointments. Why would the customer want to make an appointment? What benefit will it be to them? Do you give them a free gift or information? Is there any obligation on their part to buy? How long will it take? Did a mutual acquaintance make the referral? Tell them!

Close your sale by making the appointment. Do it in small steps: give the customer a choice of two dates and times rather than allowing him to pick a time. It may be never! You'll want to thank him for his time as well as confirm the date, time, address, and driving directions, if necessary.

Let the customer hang up first, not only because it's the polite thing to do, but also because if he has any last minute comment or question, you won't miss it! Leave a few minutes between calls in case someone is trying to reach you.

When your mini-presentation is ready, make a Call Sheet. List the names and numbers you plan to call that day alongside the best time for doing it (see chart). If you list more names than you can call under a certain time slot, schedule some for another day. Fill in blank time slots with other names from your list.

TELEPHONE TIME TABLE		
Customer type	*Morning*	*Afternoon*
Contractors	*7:00– 8:00*	*xxx*
Businesses	*9:00–11:30*	*1:30–5:00*
Office Executives	*9:00–12:00*	*2:00–5:00*
Working Class (Call at home)	*xxx*	*7:00–9:00*
Homemakers	*9:00–12:00*	*3:00–5:00*
Parents tending children	*10:00–12:00*	*12:00–1:00*
Age 60 & over	*xxx*	*1:00–4:00*
Residences	*9:00–12:00*	*12:00–9:00*

Time table for calling the right person at the
RIGHT TIME!

MAKING THE CALL

Before dialing that first phone number, quickly go over your presentations. Know what you are going to say and to whom you want to say it. Imagine the response and prepare for it. Stay flexible.

Remember to identify yourself first, and ask for the person you want to talk to. Once contact is made, identify yourself and your product, and state that you'd like to make an appointment to come and show it--it will only take twenty minutes, and there's absolutely no obligation to buy. (Or you'd like to stop by with samples and information and contact them later when they've had a chance to look it over.) If agreed to, verify name, address, and etc.

If you are caught by the "third party," the efficient secretary whose job it is to screen her employer's calls, you face a challenge! Your best bet is to make friends with her, be polite (or you'll never, ever get through) and be persistent. After countering her objections with your "yes, but" reply, repeat your request to talk to the employer. Ask her what would be a good time to call back; leave your name and number, you may get lucky and be called back out of curiosity. Be generic about your product. Sell the benefits to the secretary if you must, but create a little mystery as to just what it is. Make her your friend.

Always use your best telephone manners. Your first call is the doorway to future contact. Request time to talk--you may be interrupting something important.

Plan to work only three or four hours at a time, and take a twenty minute break every two hours. You'll need to let your phone rest for two or three minutes between calls, to let incoming calls get through (unless you have Call Holding). Never never leave someone waiting on the line while you visit with your second incoming call. Respond to the signal, quickly get a name and number, and return to the original call.

After making each appointment-setting call, write the customer's name, address, and phone number on a 3X5 card. Note also the gist of the conversation—special family members, hobbies, employment, and other interests. These will come in handy later when doing your follow-up work (see Section 3). Also note the appointment on your calendar and plan to be there on time. Take some good reading along, in case you arrive early. If you do, park a block or two away to do your waiting, then arrive no more than five minutes early.

Example: making an appointment

"Mrs. Jones? My name is Mary Smith. I'm a new WonderFace distributor, and I'm looking for WonderFace users who've lost touch with their supplier. Do you fit into that category?"
(If no, proceed to offer sample, etc.)

Example: making an appointment

"Mrs. Jones? This is Mary Smith. I'm the new WonderFace distributor for this area, and I'd like to drop by for a minute and leave you a sample and a new catalogue. Would Thursday afternoon be OK or would Friday morning be better?"

Example: making an appointment

Scene: John Cleartape sells water purifiers. He has been making calls all morning, with nothing but rejections. He considers his approach, and changes from defense to offense:

John: *"Good morning! My name is John Cleartape. Am I speaking to Mrs. Greenleaf?*

Customer: *"Yes. This is Mrs. Greenleaf."*

John: *"Did I catch you at a bad time? I'd like a few moments to talk to you about the water situation here in Appleton."*

Customer: *"What water situation?" (Now she is curious; if it was a bad time, she forgot about it.)*

John: *"Why the reservoir over at Blackwillow. Did you know the phosphates are building up in our water supply?"*

Customer: *"No," she says, "you mean we're drinking polluted water?"*

John: *"Yes, indeed, Mrs. Greenleaf. And I'd like to stop by and explain to you and Mr. Greenleaf what you can do to insure good drinking water for yourselves. Would Thursday evening at 7:30 be alright with you? It'll only take about 20 or 30 minutes."*

Customer: *"Oh yes, that would be fine. We'll be expecting you!"*

Children & Telephones

Never, never, let small children answer the telephone for a business. They must be trained in businesslike responses, and be capable of writing names and numbers correctly.

It is not a matter of losing just one customer; it is losing all the referrals that might have come from the one that got away.

GIVING THE SALES PRESENTATION

The time has come! Regardless of the location, stage fright sets in. Your pulse quickens, your hands get cold, you wonder if you can "pull it off."

Take a deep breath, exhale slowly, and remind yourself that you are not "pulling anything off." You believe in your product; do not apologize for it. You are doing the customer a favor! The customer needs your product, and you are there to help him realize that and to help in the decision to buy!

You have come equipped not only with in-depth knowledge, but also a supply of order forms, pencils, pens, blank paper, calculator, sample products, brochures, and business cards. You have practiced your presentation over and over again, until you have it memorized. You might change the wording along the way, but will stick to the formula: you'll introduce yourself, introduce your product, stress the benefits in order of importance, handle the objections, and make the sale.

No matter where your presentation is given—face-to-face, before a group, over the telephone—stick to the basic formula or content. It's 50% of your presentation. The other 50% is the way in which you give it.

Face-to-face presentations. Keep your introduction bright and confident, referring to a brochure you might have mailed, or the telephone call arranging the appointment. Hand out your business card right away, as an offer of identification.

Reaffirm the customer's name and correct pronunciation, and use it often during your presentation. While taking your position (seated at a table is best, or at the product if it is large), pass along a sincere compliment to the customer. This can be a remark about a handsome handbag or pair of shoes, an interesting piece of jewelry, or unusual home decor. Compliment the children, or a well-behaved pet. Do not overdo!

As you prepare your presentation material or product, make a mental note of the time and at what time you should be finished. Twenty or thirty minutes is ample. Now the presentation begins.

Make a note at what time you should be done.

You've already handled the introduction, so get right to the benefits. Continue on through your presentation, allowing pauses between benefits for the customer to ask questions. It will also allow you to make your appeal to the customer's senses: sight, touch, smell, taste, and hearing. Let the customer examine the product, feel it, smell it, taste it, or listen to it if applicable. Once the customer has agreed to handle or try-out the product, you are much closer to a sale.

"Let the customer examine the product, feel it, smell it, taste it, or listen to it if applicable."

Keep an eye on the customer's reactions now. You are watching for the "Hot Button," that one benefit that gets the customer's attention! When you find that, stay with it a bit longer and sell the benefits, point by point.

Watch for the customer's "hot button," the one benefit that gets special attention!

Listen intently. Eye contact is important here. Repeat and confirm any questions before answering. If the customer talks too much (some will use you as a therapist), remain diplomatic, but interrupt during a pause with something like "that's very interesting, Mrs. Greenleaf. That's one of the reasons I think you'd enjoy using..." Don't get caught up in anyone's troubles, don't gossip, and don't make a customer feel guilty for talking too much! If the customer persists in an emotional out-pouring, then offer something like "that's really a shame, Mrs. Greenleaf. I'd like to discuss it further someday when I'm not so pressed for time." This will usually get Mrs. Greenleaf back to the subject at hand and you'll have no further problems.

Counter each objection by first agreeing, then stressing the benefit or offering a solution, and asking for the order. When the sale is made, it's time to stop! Gather up your papers, thank the customer for her time and order and, as you firmly shake hands, make for the exit.

A quick parting comment on the lovely yard or a "nice meeting you" will do. Don't linger on. If pressured to visit longer by the customer, agree that you'd "like to, but" you have another appointment across town.

Group presentations.
On occasion you may
give your sales pre-
sentation before a group
or class. Use much the
same techniques as for
a face-to-face presenta-
tion.

Be sure there is a table available for your use,
and set up your display or products or brochures
before beginning the presentation. Remain at the
side or back of the room while customers are being
seated, then more briskly to the front when you are
introduced. If you will be doing your own
introduction, walk briskly to the front of the room
and command group attention by your stance: straight
and tall and knowledgeable!

Commence with your planned presentation,
speaking slowly and very clearly, as if to the very
back row in the room. Rather than pinpoint one soul
and speak only to her during your talk, scan the
room, back and forth, side to side and front to back,
making eye contact with several in the group as you
speak.

Hold off any questions or objections until a
preappointed time in your presentation, probably
following a short break, after all the benefits have
been covered.

Regrouping after the break would be a good time
to compliment them on "being such a good group,"
and then opening the floor to questions.

Repeat each question slowly and clearly, not only
to confirm that you understood it properly, but also
to allow others in the room to hear the question and
thereby not repeat it.

When all questions or objections have been met,
or when time runs out, or when the group shows
signs of restlessness, invite them to approach the
table and look over the products. If the table is
in the back of the room, you must quickly get

yourself to it, avoiding conversation unless it accompanies you to the table. Have order forms ready, pens, pencils, calculator, and try to answer all questions.

Before gathering your products and pamphlets and heading for home, make sure all orders are verified for accuracy. Thank your host, if any, and thank the group for their time. Indicate when delivery will be made, then gather together your products, etc., allowing for any last minute questions or orders. When your belongings are gathered, make your exit. Quick and clean!

Telephone presentations. Giving your sales presentation by telephone is more difficult than in person. The customer cannot see, touch, taste, or smell your product.

Only by your tone of voice can the telephone customer create an impression of you. The impression of your product is gathered by what you have to say about it. It is imperative to use descriptive words and phrases. You want to evoke feelings and visions that accurately depict your product.

"...use descriptive words and phrases... evoke feelings and visions..."

Because your contact is strictly verbal, you'll want to ask more questions. Solicit the customer's response to points you have made. Listen carefully to the answers, and indicate you are listening by an occasional "yes," "I see," "I understand," or "that's interesting." Take an interest in what the customer is saying to you while listening for tone of voice. Is the customer angry? Disturbed? Cold or distant or disinterested? Perhaps a suggestion to call back at a later date would get a successful reply.

If you reach a hostile customer, don't take it personally. Be polite and sincere. Leave the way open for a future call.

Telephone selling has its benefits. You'll save travel time and expense, save on wardrobe buying and cleaning (fewer pieces), and if you work from home, you can set your own hours! You'll get immediate responses to your presentation, and may use out-of-town directories to expand your territory and thus your business!

Mail order. When you do expand your territory, you may suddenly find yourself in the mail order business, giving your presentation on paper rather than by telephone or in person.

For this you'll need a well designed brochure, flyer, or catalog. It will show your product in use and stress the benefits as well.

Before venturing too deeply into mail order, locate a few books on the subject that will give you the inside view.

Mail order demands a lot of printing and postage and packaging. Although you should not jump into it without doing some research, it has been very rewarding to some!

Mail Order can expand your territory and increase your sales.

"An important ingredient in the successful retail or service business is good selling. Without it, many sales are lost—sales that may mean the difference between success and failure."
Small Business Administration Management Aid No. 4. 002

Do keep your voice low and slow. Add tempo to create excitement.

Do practice with a tape recorder; analyze, criticize, and improve.

Do include a "dramatic pause" in mid-sentence to draw attention to important information that will follow.

Do pause between benefits or ideas to allow the customer to ask questions.

Do vary your speed of speech between slow and medium and enthusiastic or quick!

Do listen to others and adapt what you like to your needs. Listen for speed control: a good delivery is a mixture of slow, faster, and dramatic pauses.

Do Listen to your customer; look for the need for your product.

Do help the customer visualize using and enjoying your product or service.

Do give samples, literature, compliments, or assistance--it is human nature to give back in return.

Do send articles relative to customer's hobby or other interests. It builds good will.

Do think of objections as a request for more information.

Do make notes after each presentation: what did you do right? What did you do wrong? How can you improve your presentation?

Do make notes on your 3X5 customer card about customer hobbies and other interests.

Do tell those who ask "How's business?" that you "are very busy!" People like to do business with busy, successful people!

Do show supporting evidence of the need you are filling or the claim you are making about your product. It must be from a nonbiased source.

Do maintain a positive and cheerful attitude, even in the face of rejection.

Do be diplomatic; treat customer with respect; be sympathetic to customer needs.

Do expect success with each call and presentation. Visualize it. Think of yourself as knowledgeable and confident and so will your customer.

Do behave now as what you want to be later!

> *"A life spent making mistakes is not only more honorable but more useful than a life spent doing nothing."*
> *George Bernard Shaw (1856-1950)*

Don't speak too fast, raspy, or high pitched.

Don't mumble or mispronounce words.

Don't speak so softly that you can't be easily heard.

Don't speak so loudly it hurts the customer's ears!

Don't rush your presentation, It puts too much pressure on the customer to absorb it all.

Don't ignore customer objections. Understand them, agree, and offer solution. It is not the end of the sale, but the beginning of the close.

Don't dismiss a customer that won't buy. He may be a good customer for giving you referrals.

Don't change your presentation from customer to customer. You need to judge what you do wrong or right!

Don't confuse the customer with too many facts and figures. Keep it simple, clear, & concise.

Don't forget your props for "show and tell." Show, with unbiased evidence, how good your product is.

Don't sell price only. Economy is a factor, but not everyone buys because it's cheap. Sell quality and benefits.

Don't monopolize the conversation; draw the customer into it by asking questions; find the need and fill it.

Don't pick on yourself if you don't make every sale. You have gained experience.

Don't ignore the things you did right! Compliment yourself.

Don't chew gum during your presentation.

Don't eat garlic 24 to 48 hours prior to presentation.

Don't forget: finding customers takes a lot of hard work and creativeness. The person who succeeds is the person who does the work.

"Don't wait for your ship to come in. Rent a tug & go out and meet it!"

—Author unknown

SUMMARY

1. Identify your customer. Know where they live, work, and play. Know what ages they would be, what profession or workplace and what income they must have. Who needs your product?

2. Find your customer. Use the suggestions listed in Section 2. Research at the library. Let everyone know you are in business!

3. Qualify your customer as to need, ability to pay, sincerity in buying.

4. Be prepared for drop in customers. Consider a telephone campaign to increase your territory.

5. Make appointments for giving your sales presentation or leaving information (or mailing information).Write a mini-presentation for appointment calls.Set goals for calling, make a Call Sheet indicating the best time of day to call.

6. Make the calls! Stay flexible and use good manners. Take regular breaks, and make a 3X5 card on each contact. Record appointments made on your calendar. Verify dates and times with customer.

7. Give your sales presentation! Be on time, follow suggestions for face-to-face, group, telephone, and mail order presentations.

"He who hunts for flowers will find flowers; and he who loves weeds may find weeds."
  --*Henry Ward Beecher*
  (1813-1887)

SECTION THREE: KEEP!

Presentation follow up
The follow up system
Customer service
Handling customer complaints
Summary

"Each little thing you say and do can effect in some way the image of your business...."

Finding and keeping customers is an ongoing challenge of locating, securing, maintaining, losing, and replacing.

It doesn't stop when your business is established. Some customers convert to other products, some move out of town, some fall into hard times and can't afford to patronize you, and some die. But for those that leave, others come along, and it is your work to secure them to maintain your livelihood.

That work—maintaining or keeping customers—begins with follow up. From the first Thank You, to the prompt delivery, to dependable service and repair—the various ways in which you build a customer base is endless. Each little thing you say and do can effect in some way the image of your business and whether or not people patronize it. It is a matter of being "on guard" at all times; guarding what you do, what you say, what you wear, and what you sell.

Follow up time is some of the most productive time you'll spend on your business although work you do today may not bring results for three to six months! When do you follow up? Whenever you have customer contact. Immediately following the sales presentation, for example.

PRESENTATION FOLLOW UP

To follow up after making a sale means not just delivering the product as promised, but keeping in contact on a regular basis to show the customer you care about him as an individual. That can be a short phone call to inquire about his health, or to pass along information you have found on the customer's interest or hobby. It should not always be related to your business, although you'll want to keep your customer informed as to new products or services. That can be done through phone calls or periodic mailings, like newsletters.

Follow up can bring repeat business and referrals, so consider it crucial to your business, and draw up a Follow Up Plan. It will consist of a set of goals, in logical order, for keeping in contact with your customers, and utilize the 3x5 cards you made when calling for appointments. The 3x5 system will be explained in more detail later in this section.

The **first goal** on your plan would be to make sure you have a 3x5 card for each customer, with the name, address, telephone number, and any other notes that will refresh your memory, like the number of children, special pets, hobbies, or other interests.

A friend of mine is in the insurance business and makes calls on homemakers regularly. One of his customers has an interest in fire engines, so he sends news clippings of interest when he spots them. Another of his customers is interested in nutrition and diabetes, so he watches for articles in that vein and mails them. He also does something else quite effective: he carries along a supply of stamped Thank You notes and, after completing a presentation, mails the customer a Thank You for their time, and repeats the compliment offered while he was there. His philosophy is to make friends, not customers. He is also demonstrating a genuine concern for his contacts, and his growth in business indicates it works!

Your **second goal** for the follow up plan will be to deliver the product promptly, as promised. Dependable delivery builds your integrity with the customer. If for any reason the delivery date cannot be met, you must contact the customer, apologize and explain, and allow him a choice of another two delivery dates.

Your **third goal** will be repeat contact with the customer. Telephone him in five days and ask if he has any questions, either about the product, or samples you may have left, or literature. Do not press for another sale, but let him know you'll check back in a couple of weeks.

Goal four is to call again, two weeks later. Inquire as to family health. How are they getting along with the product? Share information on a new product, and mention that you'll check with them in thirty days to see if they need anything.

The thirty-day call is **goal five.** A quick introduction (they should know who you are by this time) followed with "Do you need anything this month?" should suffice. Keep it short and non-abrasive. Friendly. If no sale, offer some quick information on a new product, and mention that you'll call again next month to see if they need anything. Your monthly follow up plan is now in effect.

The **final goal** in your plan will be to call every thirty days and ask for an order. The middle of the month is a good time to call, as the paycheck from the first of the month is usually taken with mortgage or rent payments. The second, or mid-month paycheck will have more disposable income.

In conjunction with your follow up plan, you might want to send a monthly newsletter. This can help motivate sales with special prices or services, and is not as "threatening" as verbal communication. Time its mailing to arrive the week before your monthly phone call. Newsletters and flyers need not be difficult nor expensive to make. They are an economical way to remind customers you are prepared and willing to serve them. Without constant reminders (a minimum of four times per year), the customer will revert to old habits and shop elsewhere.

Use the mail. Send Thank You's, information, samples, newsletters, flyers, coupons, holiday and anniversay remembrances or an invitation to an in-store promotion.

Sales promotions can be a good way to follow up on customers as well, but should not replace your thirty day follow up phone call.

Thanks for your time today. I enjoyed meeting you and your energetic children! Please enjoy the samples I left with you—I'll phone in a couple of weeks (few days) to see how they're working out.
Sincerely,

Thank you for coming in to look at the new Zigger Sewing machine.
I'm enclosing a brochure that explains in detail the fine Swiss engineering that makes Zigger a "stitch above" the rest!
Sincerely,

Thanks for your time today. I really enjoyed meeting you! If you have any questions about the information I left, please call me at 555-0000.
Sincerely,

You can give classes, workshops and seminars free or at a reduced fee. Hold contests, have a drawing, or organize a club. And send lots of press releases!

Your goal is to keep your name in front of the customer. Good follow up gives credibility to your business and to yourself. What you sell is yourself, your personality, your integrity, your dependability, and your attitude.

Would you do repeat business with yourself?

A monthly newsletter can help motivate sales.

THE FOLLOW UP SYSTEM

You can easily make an effective follow up system with 3x5 inch file cards (recipe cards), a set of 3x5 A-Z dividers, and a calendar. As your business grows, you may choose to expand the system, using 3x5 dividers for each month of the year, and 3x5 dividers for each day of the month. (They are available preprinted for your needs in office supply stores or mail order. See Appendix.)

The card-calendar system is simple. Make a card for each customer, as outlined earlier. After presentation, write the date, the words "sales presentation," and "call on (five days later)." Then write that customer's name on that "(five days later)" date on your calendar, and file the 3x5 card alphabetically in a 3x5 file box. You must only remember to read your calendar daily.

When day five comes, pull out any cards listed on your calendar for that date, and commence with

To start your follow-up system,
you'll want to purchase:

1. 3x5 index cards

2. 3x5 monthly dividers

3. 3x5 daily dividers

4. 3x5 file box

whatever follow up work is scheduled on each card. If "day five" or "two weeks" falls on a weekend, choose the following Monday.

When you make your follow up call, you'll have the 3x5 card in front of you, with all the notes you've made about the customer available for quick recollection.

If you get no response in two days, drop a note in the mail saying that you've been trying to reach them, and will try again at a later date. Set up your 3x5-calendar system for another week, and try again. Each time you contact a customer, note it on your 3x5 card and set a follow up date accordingly.

As your list of customers grows, you'll run out of room on the calendar for writing names. Then will be the time to expand your system.

Rather than the A-Z dividers you have been using, you'll need a set of monthly dividers, January through December, and a set of daily dividers, one through 31. You may also need a longer file box.

The expanded system works like this: customer cards are filed behind their follow up dates, behind the correct month. Each day you pull the set of cards for that day, returning the daily divider to the space behind the upcoming month.

When your follow up work is done and new follow up dates set, you simply file the customer card behind the new follow up date! It is a constant rotation of dates and months.

To get started, remove your alphabetical system and replace it with the monthly dividers. Put the upcoming month in front, with the remaining months in yearly order behind it. Place the daily dividers in front of the upcoming month, and remove the dates already gone by (put them behind next month's divider). Finally, take all customer cards out of the A-Z dividers and file them, each behind its own follow up date.

If your follow up date is more than 30 days away, simple put the card behind the proper month, and re-file behind the correct day when enough daily dividers become available.

By pulling daily a set of customer cards to contact, none of your customers will wait beyond 30 days to be served.

Looking for an "800" number?

To find out if the company you want to call has a toll-free 800 number, dial 1-800-555-1212 and ask if that company has a listing. There is no charge.

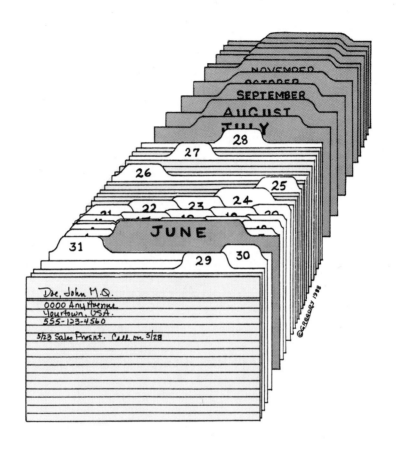

Use 3X5 cards to make a follow-up system. File customer cards behind their respective follow-up dates within the correct month. As the card is pulled for follow-up work, put the date-divider behind the last date in the upcoming month.

CUSTOMER SERVICE

What is customer service? Why is it important to your business?

Customer service, sometimes referred to as customer relations, is treating the customer in the way you would like to be treated--courteously, honestly, fairly, timely, dependably, respectfully--and doing that "little extra" favor that builds good relationships. Giving good service can mean the difference between a customer bringing repeat business or referrals to you, or taking them to the competition.

Customer service is the main ingredient of customer follow up. It begins when the sale is made, and continues for life. It can be major considerations, like delivery of and instruction on your product, or making time for customers at their convenience--before of after usual business hours.

Service can be simple things like sharing a recipe or remembering a customer's name. Your object is to build a pleasant atmosphere within your business. Your result will be many new friends who not only support your business, but also recommend it to others. Service sells!

To understand the impact of customer service first hand, do the following exercise: visit ten businesses you have never patronized (this might take a week or two). Choose a variety of subjects, like retail, service, a restaurant, and so on. Ask for information or a specific item you might be in the market for, or present an unusual request. When your visit is complete, return to your car, or home, and complete the following questionnaire before visiting another business:

CUSTOMER SERVICE FIELD TEST   Yes   No

1. Was your presence acknowledged cheerfully and quickly?   ____ ____

2. Was the first employee you encountered able to answer your question?   ____ ____

Question	Yes	No

3. Were you and your question referred to someone else to handle? _____ _____

4. Did you have to wait an uncomfortable time for service? _____ _____

5. Was the employee who answered your question courteous and confident? _____ _____

6. Did you feel pressured to buy something that did not meet your needs? _____ _____

7. Were you made to feel that your problem was unimportant? _____ _____

8. Was there an offer to follow up? _____ _____

9. Were YOU asked to follow up? _____ _____

10. Did you feel that your business was welcomed? _____ _____

11. If a phone call or delivery was to be made, was it on time as promised? _____ _____

12. Did employees remain positive that they could help with your needs? _____ _____

13. Were you thanked for your patronage? _____ _____

14. Were prices marked openly on goods, or did you have to ask? _____ _____

15. Was your personal check or credit card accepted without complaint? _____ _____

16. Were you treated the way you'd like to be treated? _____ _____

17. Would you do business there again? _____ _____

18. Would you recommend that business to your friends? _____ _____

OFFICE HOURS OF SMALL BUSINESSOWNERS

Open most days about 9:00 or 10:00, occasionally as early as 7:00, but some days as late as 12:00 or 1:00.

We close about 5:30 or 6:00, sometimes as late as 11:00 or 12:00.

Some afternoons we aren't here at all. Lately I've been here just about all the time, except when I'm someplace else, but I should be here then, too.

author unknown

*(Borrowed from Barbara Brabec's **National Home Business Report**)*

After your visits of investigation, it will be clear where businesses are falling short in terms of customer service.

It will also be clear what appeals to you, and that will help you decide what your policies will be under similar circumstances. It's good to devise some basic policies, although often you'll encounter the unexpected, and have to make on-the-spot decisions. A short list of policies, not cast in concrete, is especially helpful to employees.

Although they must be taught to stay flexible, like you, employees need to know their role. How much authority do they have? What decisions can they make in your absence? What do you expect of them in terms of loyalty, attitude, product knowledge, and customer service?

A well trained employee is also a service to your customer. You are the one that will instill confidence of your product, confidence in your business, and confidence in yourself. Your conviction, your actions, and your reactions, all become part of your employee's attitude and belief in your business. Without that belief and confidence, they cannot project the same to the customer.

It is your responsibility to see that all employees are properly trained. A clerk turned loose on the sales floor can lose you a sale and perhaps future sales by something as trivial as not understanding how your telephone system works!

Employees need to know of special discounts or coupons, and and limitations put on them. They need to know your policy of accepting personal checks or credit cards, and how to handle a layaway purchase.

They need to know your philosophy of greeting customers and answering the telephone. Do you want you calls screened? Show them how to do it politely!

If errors are made, you will need to correct and retrain. Do it in private. Never in front of customers, and never in front of other employees. Public humiliation may make you feel like "the boss," but the end result is that the entire business loses credibility.

Customers not only lose confidence in the employee and in your business as a whole, but are forced into the middle of a very uncomfortable situation. They will not hurry back to risk it again!

Employees are people too. The **Golden Rule** applies to them as well as to customers!

The old adage "good help is hard to find" is more truth than habit. Good employees need motivation to keep putting in the hours. Wages aren't the only factor. Keep them happy with good working conditions--a clean and safe workplace, regular breaks, discounts, paid vacations, bonus incentives, and lots of praise. Never criticize or correct without offering a compliment as well. Employees need to know what you expect and need from them, and good behavior should be reinforced with praise for a job well done!

Involve employees with company promotions. Planning and organizing a promotion gives the employee a real sense of belonging, not to mention a sense of accomplishment and enthusiasm for the business. It also takes some of the work off your shoulders, and you shouldn't complain about that!

Example: Policies & Procedures List

1. Walk-in and telephone customers will be acknowledged quickly and cheerfully by name (unless unknown).

2. Prices on merchandise will be openly marked, allowing the customer to relate to his budget without feeling pressured.

3. Personal checks will be accepted with two pieces of identification: a current driver's license and a major credit card. (This might be waived for regular buyers)

4. A layaway option will be available to all customers: one third down, one third in two weeks, and one third in 30 days.

5. Accounts receivable (if any): 30 days net. (Work with a past due customer rather than lose the account; suggest a small payment plan; follow up on it).

6. No gossiping in the store.

7. The telephone will be answered promtply and courteously; no long holding; check back frequently; offer to call back. A telephone customer will not take preference over an in-store one.

8. The answering machine will be turned on at closing time (message will give store name and business hours).

9. Personal calls must be short and informative.

10. The receptionist will be kept informed of company policies, whereabouts of owners.

11. Customer purchases will be gift wrapped and delivered, if requested.

12. Regular customers will be notified in advance of price increases.

A Field Test: The Restaurant

It was a sunny day during strawberry season when my husband and I visited a nearby restaurant, anxious for our first fresh strawberry shortcake of the season.

My husband was using crutches at the time, and it was with great difficulty we opened the heavy wooden doors to enter. This was out first venture into a public place since his amputation.

A waitress greeted us almost instantly, and, seeing our disability, asked if we would be more comfortable in the dining room of the establishment. We agreed, and cautiously made our way past a few diners to seat ourselves.

The waitress continued her attention with a quick "I'll be right there!" and "would you folks like coffee?"

She noted our approval, and rushed away with an "I'll be right back!"

We adjusted our chairs, crutches, and jackets. And waited for the coffee. And waited. And waited. And waited. I figure it takes about seven minutes to realize that one has been forgotten, but we gave her the benefit of the doubt, and waited a few minutes longer. The strawberry shortcake would be so very good!

Seven minutes lagged into fifteen, then twenty. It was too much! I ventured around the corner of the room to the counter, to ask if the coffee was coming. As I approached the counter, there stood our waitress, wiping the counter and discussing last night's date with another waitress. I had to wait until the conversation was completed before gaining any acknowledgement.

Reluctantly she plodded to the cups, to the coffee pot, and finally to our table. We stayed and paid **only** because of the great difficulty in entering another restaurant! We have never been back.

Was that waitress doing the owner a favor? Was she giving customer service? Will we recommend that restaurant to our friends?

I think you know the answer!

A Field Test: The Sales Staff & the Telephone

One of my "test" visits was to the drug store. I hurried in to pick up a roll of film to take along on an interview I was doing that day. Just one little roll of film, black and white, for which I was ready to pay cash. Quick and clean!

Only one customer was in line for the cashier. Good! I proffered my roll of film and had my cash at the ready, when the telephone rang. The cashier answered the telephone and rang up my purchase at the same time. I was impressed! How efficient!

Not true, as it turns out. The cashier drops the "action" part of my transaction, and gets involved in a long conversation about something she evidently was not trained to handle.

I waited. And waited. And, as is the case with such customer service, the longer I waited the more frustrated and angry I became. Was I to be late for my appointment due to her lack of service? Will I hurry to return to that store again? Will I send my friends?

Telephone receptionists **must** be trained in how to handle every situation, to know what authority they have and have not, to know where each and every inquiry should be transferred. Unless it is a dire emergency, an incoming call **should not** take precedence over a cash customer waiting to pay!

Policies & Procedures Points to Consider:

Business hours: must be stable and dependable.

Telephone answering: must be courteous & helpful.

Accounts receivable: will you accept credit cards, and/or carry accounts yourself?

Layaway: set a standard for amount of down payment (percentage of purchase) and payoff-pickup date. Will you refund layaway deposits?

Return checks: how will you collect them? How will you avoid accepting them? What ID will you require?

Merchandise returns: When will they be allowed? Will you refund cash or credit toward other merchandise?

Complaints: how will you handle them?

Training employees: what do you expect of them? How much authority will you give them?

Other: what other situations might you encounter?

> "Let the customer expound.
> Let the anger be released.
> Get the facts, listen.
> A happy customer is your
> best customer!

HANDLING CUSTOMER COMPLAINTS

No matter how courteous you are, no matter how well trained your employees, no matter how perfect your product is, you will get complaints.

They run the gamut from small and silly to large litigations. For the large litigation type, see your attorney. And make sure from the start that you are fully insured.

For the small and silly, adjustments to keep a customer happy can usually be made. The process is not unlike handling objections in your sales presentation.

First you agree--either that you admit the error, or you agree that they feel the way they do. Let the customer expound. Let the anger be released.

Get the facts; listen very carefully. Repeat the problem as you understand it, for verification. Then explain what you can and cannot do, and give the customer a choice of solutions. Offer an alternative, a refund, a motion to go out of your way to please the customer. Do it cheerfully and quickly.

A happy customer is your best customer. He will return with repeat business and send referrals.

You hope those referrals will all be happy customers too. Occasionally, however, you will get a "weed." Like the tending of your flower garden

(Section 2), the weed must be plucked from the ground--gently but firmly--soas not to disturb the fine flowers that surround it.

Weeds come in all shapes and sizes, and are not always easy to identify. Some write bad checks, some "borrow" merchandise and return it for credit or cash, some merely come to visit--to share their daily problems. Some mishandle your merchandise or let their children run wildly throughout your store! How do you get rid of them?

The flower garden is an everchanging, exciting renewal of life. But, occasionally you have to pull a weed.

You be creative. You be diplomatic. You be determined in your course of action, but cautious to not discredit your business by openly accusing or rebuffing.

You can cut back on customer service, ignore, ostracize, or not accept checks or credit cards. You must consider the price of "pulling the weed" compared to referrals you might get.

I once "pulled a weed" by letter. She was constantly "borrowing" clothing from my apparel shop, then returning it some weeks later, permeated with perfume. She wanted cash in return. Maybe a large department store could absorb that. I could not! It called for additional investment (dry cleaning) into a used garment!

She was a pro at her craft, always accompanied by a friend upon returning, or ready to create a scene in front of other valuable customers if she didn't get her way. I became determined to stop her; and I did.

Upon her last return request, I insisted that a

refund of that amount required it be made by check, and I was too busy with business that day to issue it. With her approval, I promised I would mail it. And I did. And enclosed it in a letter that said something to the effect of "...inasmuch as your patronage has never been satisfactory to either of us, I urge you to henceforth shop for your apparel needs elsewhere." She never entered my store again! Sometimes, customers need to know what we expect of them, too.

Experience has a lot to do with learning to deal with unwanted customers. To tap into a wealth of business experience, contact a few organizations existing for that purpose!

The Small Business Administration puts out a lot of good books and pamphlets for managing small business. You can order them through the mail (see Appendix for address). Call your local Small Business Administration office and ask about workshops you can attend.

Call local banking institutions and ask for advice or a schedule of their small business seminars.

Community colleges are another resource for helpful programs for small business.

Check your local telephone directory for a Small Business Resource Center and find out what they can offer you.

Attend Chamber of Commerce meetings and learn how your participation can benefit your business.

And refer to the many resources listed in the appendix of this book.

"Service sells. Always has, always will. "

--*Jim Cleland*
Seattle businessman

CHAMBER OF COMMERCE

What can a Chamber of Commerce do for its members?

"Give them support, for one thing," says June Cornett. "By attending meetings, business owners and managers can share in each others' experiences. They can build a network of friendships that offer support not found elsewhere in the entrepreneurial world!"

Members will gain knowledge, too. They can partake in fact-filled seminars and plug their emotional drains with encouragement from motivational speakers.

June serves on the Marketing Committee of her local Chamber of Commerce. "We plan events to attract shoppers," she says. "Economic development for the community is the purpose of a Chamber of Commerce."

That can be accomplished through a variety of methods, according to June. "The Quality of Life Committee, for example," she reports, "sponsors family and sporting events.

"By supporting or sponsoring art fairs, concerts, holiday activities and pageants that attract visitors from surrounding areas, both businesses and family life benefit."

"Ultimately, with creative planning, economic development can enrich all phases of community life."

June Cornett is a writer and producer of brochures. You can reach her at June's Professional Services, Inc., P.O.Box 269, Edmonds, WA 98020.

Customer Relations: The Discount Shopper

In the day-to-day operation of a retail store, you will get the customer who prides himself on never paying full price.

Being a small business owner, you know how very hard it is to make a dollar; in fact how hard it is just to pay the rent at times! The public doesn't know this. They believe that **all** retailers "have it made."

It has been my fortune to meet a retailer with a keen sense of timing and all the right replies on command. She owns a gift shop stocked with fine crystal, collectible dolls, figurines, and the like.

Her discount shopper was a burly, "bull-in-the-china-shop" type. He studied a large crystal vase, then snarled, "When's this gonna be half price?"

Astutely aware of this ploy for a discount, my friend raised her eyes to his, in her best Cocker Spaniel gaze. "I'm sorry, Sir. Are you out of work?"

"No!" came the defensive response, "I'm a dock worker—I been workin full time! Make real good money, too Lady."

"Would you do the same work for half your current wages?" she innocently inquired.

"No Mam! We've worked darned hard for our wages; there's no reason I should work for half!"

"Well, Sir," she continued, "you're asking me to cut my prices in half for you. Don't you think that reduces any profit that might be left for me? Why sometimes I don't even get a paycheck—and I work a good sixty hours a week!"

He didn't get the crystal. But I'm sure he did get a better vision of the small retailer's situation.

SUMMARY

1. Develop and stick to a follow-up plan. Start by making a 3X5 file card on each and every contact. Call in five days; call again two weeks after that; call again thirty days after that; then call monthly. Mail newsletters or flyers to all customers on a regular basis, especially if operating a retail shop where telephone follow-up is not plausible.

2. Use your 3X5 file cards as a follow-up system. File either alphabetically with call dates noted on your calendar, or file under month and date to be called.

3. Create policies and procedures that encourage good customer service. Make a first hand "field test" of ten businesses to help determine what you will do differently. Train your employees accordingly, and know that you are responsible for their training and ultimately their success with your customers!

4. Handle customer complaints like you would handle an objection during your sales presentation. Make adjustments when necessary; terminate your association when necessary.

5. Tap into others' experience by contacting the Small Business Administration, local banking institutions, community colleges, the Small Business Resource Center, and your Chamber of Commerce.

APPENDIX

Resources: Associations, Books,
        Classes & Seminars, Magazines,
        Newsletters, Suppliers

Library Research Guide

Eleven Ways to Create Profit-Making
        Advertising by Robert Serling

Follow up suggestions for 38 businesses

The Press Release

Making Newsletters

The Cycle of Business

RESOURCES

The associations, books, classes and seminars, magazines, newsletters, and suppliers names and addresses herein are listed as a courtesy and convenience. The reader is expected to employ consumer awareness when dealing with any mail order firm.

HOW TO USE THE LISTS

Associations. Write or call ones that sound applicable to your business. Ask for a brochure describing goals, benefits, dues, and etc.

Books. Listed by catagory. First seek the books of your choice at your local library. The ISBN number (International Standard Book Number) has been listed for help in ordering titles from bookstores (check the price before ordering, or ask if you can order it "on approval.") If not available through your bookstore, write to the publisher.

Classes & Seminars. Write or call for more information. Also, contact your local Small Business Administration, the Small Business Resource Center, the Chamber of Commerce, the Community College, and local banks for news of small business workshops.

Magazines. Write for a sample copy and subscription information. Also, by separate letter, request a "Media Kit." (See sample letter).

Newsletters. Write for subscription information and a sample copy. Small business newsletters may be condensed information, gleaned from larger publications or experts in the field, or shared experiences of fellow small business owners across the country.

Suppliers. Write for a catalog. Compare prices.

When requesting infor-
mation by mail, always
include a SASE -- self-
addressed, stamped,
envelope.

SAMPLE LETTER: REQUEST FOR MEDIA KIT

L E T T E R H E A D

Date

Magazine Name
Advertising Department
Publisher's address
City, State Zip

Ladies & Gentlemen:

I would like to consider your publication as an advertising medium
for my product.   Please forward a media package, including:

        1. Classified and display rates

        2. Circulation figures

        3. Readership demographics

        4. Editorial schedule

        5. Sample copies

Thank you.

YOUR COMPANY NAME

Your signature here.

Your name, Title

What can a Media Kit do for you? In addition to learning classified and display ad costs, you will be able to review a copy of the magazine for content and current advertisers. You can study the circulation and demographic information to determine if it meets your target audience, and you can locate names of department and editors for mailing your press releases.

ASSOCIATIONS

The purpose of any association listed hereunder is a direct quote from information supplied by that association, and not the opinion of the author or publisher.

American Association for Adult and Continuing Education, 1112 - 16th Street N W, Suite 420, Washington, DC 20036. (202)463-6333. PURPOSE: "non-profit education association whose mission is to advance research and practice in the field, and to advocate for it."

American Federation of Small Business, 407 South Dearborn, Chicago, IL 60608. (312)427-0209. PURPOSE: "to help our members with any business problem, and prevent government granted monopolies, whether by taxation, regulation, credit, or labor laws."

Handweavers Guild of America, 120 Mountain Avenue, Bloomfield, CT 06013. (203)242-3577. PURPOSE: "to inspire creativity and to promote participation in and appreciation of the fiber arts."

Independent Computer Consultants Association, 933 Gardenview Office Parkway, St. Louis, MO 63141. (314)997-4633 or (800)GET-ICCA. PURPOSE: "provide support and benefits to members and availability of services to consumer public."

National Retail Merchants Association, 100 West 31st Street, New York, NY 10001.

Small Business Administration, P.O. Box 15434, Ft. Worth, TX 76116.

The National Writers Club, 1450 South Havana, Suite 620, Aurora, CO 80012. (303)751-7844. PURPOSE: "we are a national support base and information service for freelance writers."

The Perfect Life Connection, 2001 East Locust Court, Ontario, CA 91761. (714)947-6637. PURPOSE: "an organization for distributors and franchisees and consumer members, providing a wide range of health services, nutritional products, and consumer benefit programs."

BOOKS: ADVERTISING, PROMOTION, PUBLICITY

Chase's Calendar of Annual Events by William D. & Helen Chase. ISSN 0740-5286

How to Advertise & Promote Your Retail Store by Dana K. Cassell (American Management Assoc., NY).

Marketing without Advertising by Michael Phillips & Salli Rasberry (NOLO Press) ISBN 0-87337-019-8.

The Publicity Manual by Kate Kelly (Visibility Enterprises, 11 Rockwood Drive, Larchmont, NY 10538). ISBN 0-9603740-1-9.

How to make Newsletters, Brochures, & Other Good Stuff without a computer system by H. Gregory (Pinstripe Publishing, POBox 711, Sedro-Woolley, WA 98284) ISBN 0-941973-01-8.

Editing Your Newsletter by Mark Beach (Coast to Coast Books, 2934 N.E. 16th Avenue, Portland, Oregon 97212) ISBN 0-943381-01-0.

BOOKS: CATALOGS & DIRECTORIES

Directory of Mail Order Catalogs (Grey House Publishing, Pocket Knife Square, Lakeville, CT 06039) ISBN 0-939300-05-2.

The Bookseller (JEB Publications, P.O.Box 19036, Chicago, IL 60619). Catalog.

Jeffrey Lant's Sure-Fire Business Success Catalog (Jeffrey Lant Associates, 50 Follen Street, Suite 507, Cambridge, MA 02138).

BOOKS: CRAFTS BUSINESS

Creative Cash—Making Money with your Crafts, Needlework, Designs and know-how by Barbara Brabec (Barbara Brabec Productions, P.O.Box 2137, Naperville, IL 60566).

Crafts Marketing Success Secrets by Barbara Brabec (Barbara Brabec Productions, P.O.Box 2137, Naperville, IL 60566).

How to Start your own Craft Business by Herb Genfan and Lyn Taetzsch (Watson-Guptill Publications, New York). ISBN 0-8230-2470-9.

BOOKS: CUSTOMER RELATIONS

Customer Education by Claudia G. Meer. (Nelson-Hall). ISBN 0-8304-1049-X.

How to Handle Customer Complaints by Chris Moore (Gower Publishing Co) ISBN 0-7161-0263-3.

How to Handle Major Customers Profitably by Alan V. Melkman (Gower Publishing Co) ISBN 0-566-02097-1.

Increasing Your Sales through Customer Services: A Critical Function in Transition by Fred S. Rosenau and Leslie R. Chase. ISBN 0-942774-15-09.

Swim with the Sharks—Without Being Eaten Alive! by Harvey McKay (William Morrow & Co)

BOOKS: DRESSING & BODY LANGUAGE

Dress for Success by John T. Molloy.

Glamour's Success Book: Effective Dressing on the Job, at Home, in the Community, Everywhere by Barbara Coffey and the Editors of Glamour. (Fireside, S&S) ISBN 0-671-46263-6.

Manwatching. A Field Guide to Human Behavior by Desmond Morris (Abrams) ISBN 0-8109-2184-7.

The Woman's Dress for Success Book by John T. Molloy.

BOOKS: HOME BASED BUSINESS

Help for your Growing Homebased Business by Barbara Brabec (Barbara Brabec Productions, P.O.Box 2137, Naperville, IL 60566).

How to make your Homebased Business Grow: Getting Bigger Profits from your Products by Valerie Bohigian (NAL) ISBN 0-452256-20-8.

Homemade Money — The Definitive Guide to Success in a Home Business by Barbara Brabec (Barbara Brabec Productions, P.O.Box 2137, Naperville, IL 60566).

Profitable Part-Time Home Based Businesses by Gary Null (Pilot Books) ISBN 0-87576-030-9.

Working at Home by Hannah C. McGarity (Mrs. H.C. McGarity, P.O.Box 200504, Cartersville, GA 30120).

BOOKS: MANAGEMENT

Growing a Business by Paul Hawken (Fireside, S&S) ISBN 0-67164-2.

How to Manage a Retail Store by J. Wingate and S. Helfant (Coles Publishing).

Small Time Operator by Bernard Kamoroff (Bell Springs Pub.) ISBN 0-917510-06-2.

Starting & Managing the Small Business by Arthur Kuriloff, John Hemphill Jr. (McGraw) ISBN 0-07-035662-9.

Payment in Full: A Guide to Successful Bill Collecting
by Leonard Bendell (Triad, 1110 N.W. 8th Ave, Gainesville, FL 32601)

BOOKS: SELF CONFIDENCE, VISUALIZATION

As a Man Thinketh by James Allen (G.P.Putnam's Sons, NY) ISBN 0-399-12829-8.

How to Develop Self-Confidence and Influence People by Public Speaking by Dale Carnegie. ISBN 0-671-54435-7.

How to Win Friends & Influence People by Dale Carnegie. ISBN 0-671-49408-2.

The Power of your Subconscious Mind by Dr. Joseph Murphy (Prentice-Hall, Inc) ISBN 0-13-685925-9.

BOOKS: SELLING

Never Underestimate the Selling Power of a Woman by Dottie Walters (Wilshire Book Co, 12015 Sherman Road, North Hollywood, CA 91605) ISBN 0-87980-416-5.

Successful Telephone Selling in the 80's by Martin D. Shafiroff and Robert L. Shook (Harper & Row, NY) ISBN 0-06-014952-3.

Telephone Techniques that Sell by Charles Bury (Warner Books, Inc, NY) ISBN 0-446-38097-0.

The Unabashed Self Promoter's Guide by Jeffrey Lant (JLA Publications, 50 Follen Street, Suite 507, Cambridge, MA 02138) ISBN 0-940374-06-4.

Winning through Intimidation by Robert J. Ringer (Fawcett Crest Books) ISBN 0-449-20786-2.

CLASSES, SEMINARS

"Making a living without a job," **"Establish yourself as an expert,"** **"Mostly Mail Order,"** **"Cheap tricks: Marketing on a shoestring,"** and **"Creating Newsletters"** are currently being held in Minnesota, California, and Connecticut. Interested in getting one in your area? Contact: Barbara J. Winter, P.O.Box 35412, Minneapolis, MN 55435.

"Information Marketing Success," and **"Mail Order Success."** For schedules and locations, contact Russ von Hoelscher, P. O. Box 546, El Cajon, CA 92022.

MAGAZINES

Business Network (Minnesota small business)
P. O. Box 232
Cambridge, MN 55008

Entrepreneur Magazine
2311 Pontius Avenue
Los Angeles, CA 90064

Home Business Advisor
NextStep Publications
P. O. Box 41108
Fayetteville, NC 28309

In Business Magazine
Box 323
Emmaus, PA 18049

Income Opportunities Magazine
Davis Publications, Inc.
380 Lexington Avenue
New York, NY 10017

New Business Opportunities Magazine
P. O. Box 870
Largo, FL 34649-0870

New Families
NextStep Publications
P. O. Box 41108
Fayetteville, NC 28309

Opportunity Magazine
6 North Michigan Avenue
Chicago, IL 60602

The Crafts Report
700 Orange Street
Wilmington, DE 19801

Success Magazine
HAL Publications
342 Madison Avenue
New York, NY 10173

NEWSLETTERS

National Home Business Report
Barbara Brabec Productions
P. O. Box 2137
Naperville, IL 60566

Pairs, A Newsletter for Couples in Business
Self Employment Consultants
1090 Cambridge Street
Novato, CA 94947

Shoestring Marketer Newsletter
Ad Mail Management
P. O. Box 1389
Yuba City, CA 95992-1389

The Business Owner
Thomar Publications, Inc.
383 South Broadway
Hicksville, NY 11801

Winning Ways News
Winning Ways Press
P. O. Box 35412
Minneapolis, MN 55435

Working at Home
P. O. Box 200504
Cartersville, GA 30120

SUPPLIERS (OFFICE & PACKAGING)

Atlas Pen & Pencil Corp.
3040 North 29th Avenue
Hollywood, FL 33022

Avery International Co.
777 East Foothill Blvd.
Azusa, CA 91702

Chiswick Trading, Inc.
33 Union Avenue
Sudbury, MA 01776-0907

Consolidated Plastics Co.
1864 Enterprise Parkway
Twinsburg, Ohio 44087

Fidelity Products Co.
P. O. Box 155
Minneapolis, MN 55440-0155

NEBS
New England Business Services
500 Main Street
Groton, MA 01471

Quill Corporation
100 South Schelter Road
Lincolnshire, IL 60069-9585

Rapidforms
501 Benigno Blvd.
Bellmawr, NJ 08031-9886

Sno King Rubber Stamp
P. O. Box 626
Lynnwood, WA 98046

The Business Book
One East 8th Avenue
Oshkosh, WI 54901

The Printers Shopper
P. O. Drawer 1056
Chula Vista, CA 92012

20th Century Plastics
3628 Crenshaw Blvd.
Los Angeles, Ca 90016

Viking Office Products
P. O. Box 61144
Los Angeles, Ca 90061-0144

LIBRARY RESEARCH GUIDE

Some books are to be tasted, others to be
swallowed, and some few to be chewed and digested. "
--Lord Veralam Francis Bacon (1561-1626)

©GREGORY 1988

An unending feast of knowledge waits within the walls of your local library. You can select from a menu so large it's on microfiche, or thumb through the card catalog system for your particular craving.

Your maitre d'library is happy to help you make a selection, and generally insists upon doing the cleanup when you are through!

You may borrow a few "specialties of the house" to digest at your leisure, and IT'S ALL FREE!

Can't afford a book you want? Give the information to your librarian, and request that the library purchase a copy. The library needs to know what kinds of books you want to read!

If you haven't been to the library for awhile, you've got some exciting changes in store! What do you do first? Here's a guide that will help you in your search:

1. Prepare yourself beforehand with a pad and pencil or pen. A steno pad works well, and you can clip a ballpoint pen inside the spiral binding for quick access.

2. Make a list on your pad of the subject matter or items you want to research. Note them in as many terms and applications as you can--by what other name could they be called?

For example, if you are researching for a Yarn Shop, you will want to check not only yarn, but knitting, crocheting, fiber arts, weaving, stitchery, and wool and other fibers. Women's apparel might also be found under clothing, garments, costuming, designer wear, and so on.

3. Once inside the library, you'll want to ask the librarian three things:

(a) Where the **Reference Section** is located. Here you will find books used for quick information gathering. They are not loaned out, and include encyclopedias, dictionaries, almanacs, directories, and general reference books.

(b) Where the **Card Catalog** system is located, and
(c) how the **Microfiche** system works. The microfiche and card catalog systems list books your library (or library system) has available. From these two sources, you can locate titles and authors of books in your subject area, and find out where they will be shelved in your library--by the Dewey Decimal System number or the Library of Congress classification letter. You'll notice that the shelves of books (called "stacks"), are labeled with one or the other.

Suppose you want to find the book <u>Dress for Success</u> by John T. Molloy. You'll note a decimal number, such as 646.32, on the microfiche listing. First you find the stack holding the 600 numbers, then follow it along until you reach the 640's, then specifically look for 646.32 until you identify the book.

Dewey Decimal System

000 General works	500 Natural Science
100 Philosophy	600 Useful Arts
200 Religion	700 Fine Arts
300 Social Science	800 Literature
400 Language	900 History

Library of Congress Classification

A General works
B Philosophy, Psychology, Religion
C Auxiliary Sciences, History
D History, general & old
E History, U.S., general
F History, U.S., Canada, Latin America
G Geography
H Social Science
K Law
L Education
M Music, books on music
N Fine Arts
P Language, Literature
Q Science
R Medicine
S Agriculture
T Technology
U Military Science
V Naval Science
Z Bibliography, Library Science

---

4. To locate other books not in your library system, or books you may wish to order from a book store, check under subject matter, title, or author in the volumes called **Books in Print.** Most often you will need to ask the librarian for them. Note the title, author, publisher, and ISBN number for ordering.

5. To find magazine and newspaper articles on your subject matter, look through the series of books titled **Reader's Guide to Periodical Literature.** It will give you the magazine title, issue, and page on which the article appears. In addition, you will find other magazine article information listed in an index called **Access.**

OTHER REFERENCE MATERIAL

In addition to encyclopedias, directories, general reference books and publications listing books and articles, there are books listing sources of information, called "indexes."

To determine if your library has a particular directory or index, check the microfiche or card catalog. A few are included in the following list of Other Reference Material.

Addresses
Reverse directories
Area and out-of-town telephone directories

Associations
ENCYCLOPEDIA OF ASSOCIATIONS
DIRECTORY OF ASSOCIATIONS

Arts, Crafts, & Design
ART INDEX (H.W.Wilson Company)
INDEX TO HOW-TO-DO-IT INFORMATION
   (Norman Lathrop Enterprises)

Business
BUSINESS INDEX (Information Access Corp.)
BUSINESS PERIODICALS INDEX (H.W.Wilson Co.)
ENCYCLOPEDIA OF BUSINESS INFORMATION SOURCES
(Gale Research)

Directories
DIRECTORY OF DIRECTORIES

Food & Nutrition
NUTRITION ABSTRACTS & REVIEWS (Commonwealth Agricultural Bureau & John Wiley & Sons)

Opinion
THE GALUP POLL
CONSUMER'S INDEX TO PRODUCT EVALUATIONS
   & INFORMATION SOURCES (Pierian Press)

Promotion Planning
CHASE'S CALENDAR OF ANNUAL EVENTS

Science
GENERAL SCIENCE INDEX (H.W.Wilson Co.)

Statistics
AMERICAN STATISTICS INDEX (ASI) for Federal
and State statistics.
STATISTICAL REFERENCE INDEX (SRI) for pub-
lishers, associations, and business statistics.
STATISTICAL YEARBOOK (United Nations, Department
of International Economic & Social Affairs: Statistical
Office) for statistics from foreign countries.

Trade Magazines
LITERARY MARKET PLACE
MAGAZINE INDUSTRY MARKET PLACE
WRITERS DIGEST

Trade names, American manufacturers
TRADE NAMES DICTIONARY (Gale Research Co.)
THOMAS REGISTER OF AMERICAN MANUFACTURERS

U.S.Government
INDEX TO U.S.GOVERNMENT PERIODICALS

QUICK TRIP TO THE LIBRARY?

1. Take along paper, pencil, and subject matter notes.

2. Go directly to the Reference Section.

3. Search the encyclopedias under subject matter. Take notes.

4. Search for relevant books under subject matter classification (LC or Dewey Decimal system). Take notes!

5. Search the bibliography in books you find for other books on the subject.

6. Borrow appropriate books from the regular check-out section for home study. Search their bibliographies for other titles.

7. Mail your question on most any subject to:
LIBRARY OF CONGRESS
ATTN: Head, Referral
    Services Section
Washington, DC 20540

Enclose a SASE (self-addressed, stamped, envelope) and your question will be forwarded to an appropriate organization for reply.

NOTES

ELEVEN WAYS TO CREATE PROFIT-MAKING ADVERTISING

1. Target your audience. Be as specific as possible. Selling to a specialized group has a far greater chance of succeeding than trying to appeal to everyone. To maximize profits, make the right offer to the right audience.

2. Grab your prospects' attention. To do this, you need a headline that SCREAMS an immediate benefit to your prospects. A benefit so useful, they can't possibly resist being drawn into your sales piece.

3. Solve your customers' most irritating problems. This is the key to successful advertising. There's no more effective way to sell than to demonstrate your ability to make your customers' lives easier, better, or more worry free.

4. Use the key word every customer wants to hear — YOU. Use it over and over again. To motivate customers to part with their hard-earned dollars, you have to speak to them directly and personally. And show that you understand their needs. The best way to do this, and to get your customers to identify with your message, is to use "you" language.

5. Focus on benefits, not features. Let's say you're a CPA going into business for yourself. Your sales literature lists all of the accounting services you provide -- bookkeeping, tax preparation, payroll services. But what do these services DO for your customers? Save them time, money, or make accurate tracking of costs a breeze? Focusing on benefits helps you drive home how your product or service will improve customers' lives.

6. Avoid using too much jargon. Insider language limits your audience to the few people who already understand your specialized terminology. It also puts prospects off by coming across as stiff and formal. Unless you want to appeal to a highly limited group of specialists, go easy on the jargon.

7. Keep your message clear and simple. Focus on one or two major benefits. Shorten your sentences for extra punch. And try to keep your paragraphs to a maximum of four sentences.

8. Making a claim? Prove it! A major stumbling block for most advertisers is getting prospects to believe you can deliver what you promise. Be specific with your proof. 16,184 sounds more believable than "over 15,000." Another winning point— use testimonials to show prospects how you've successfully helped others just like them.

9. Respect your customers. Don't insult them with puffed up, extravagant claims. Today's consumers demand sincere, believable information presented in a way that respects their dignity.

10. Tell your customers—clearly and directly—what you want them to do. Don't be shy. Tell them to clip your coupon and send in their order, or to request your free brochure today. If you don't tell your customers exactly what to do, and more than once, they probably won't do anything.

11. Get help from a professional when you need it. Writing advertising copy can be a difficult chore. And ineffective copy wastes a lot of time, effort, and money. You can avoid this by investing in the services of a professional.

--Robert Serling

Robert Serling is a Los Angeles based marketing consultant. He specializes in creating hard hitting, persuasive advertising and developing profit making marketing plans. He can be reached at 3960 Laurel Canyon Boulevard, Suite 380, Studio City, California 91604. Telephone (818)761-2952. "Eleven Ways to Create Profit-Making Advertising" reprinted by permission.

FOLLOW UP SUGGESTIONS FOR SOME BUSINESSES

Accountants: Mail a quarterly newsletter to all clients, advising new strategies in tax planning, etc.

Apparel shops: Men's, women's, or children's. Send flyers at least quarterly advising of specials; include coupons with expiration date. Make phone calls to certain customers when special new arrival received in their size and color. Offer alterations.

Antique dealers: Send newsletters or flyers regularly to customers. Follow up special orders with phone calls. Include "collectible" information in your newsletter such as current values, care and restoration techniques, etc. Hold an Open House yearly.

Auto dealers: The service department must send reminders for periodic service; send flyers or coupon sheets for special prices on tune ups, parts and labor. Sales department can watch daily repair orders for possible replacement needs; call previous buyers quarterly to check on buyer satisfaction and ask for referrals.

Bakeries: Send flyers to churches, clubs, business organizations offering special price/delivery on baked goods, catering, etc. Send business card or brochure to wedding consultants, advising what benefits your bakery can give.

Catering, cooking: Place small ad in local weekly paper; contact churches, clubs, business organizations, Bed & Breakfast Inns as well as previous customers.

Charter services: Aircraft, boat, bus: mail or phone large companies that entertain--tourist and convention bureaus. Mail flyers or newsletters to prior clients, advising season schedule ahead of time. (If applicable)

Beauty salons: Make six week phone call or mail reminder to present clients; take Yellow Pages ad.

Bed & Breakfast: Send yearly mailer to previous guests; quarterly flyers to travel agencies; prepare "keepsake" booklet to give to guests; send press releases regularly to appropriate magazines, include black and white glossy.

Boat care & repair: Hand out business cards; post at marina; prepare pamphlet on services, benefits; phone previous clients to ask for referrals.

Bookkeeper: Send quarterly newsletter to clients; include bookkeeping tips, updates on systems, etc; ask for referrals.

Children's Party Clown: Carry business cards with photo; send favors and flyer home with party goers; take Yellow Pages ad; Use phone campaign to previous customers to ask for referrals, advise new entertainment, etc.

Color consultant: Mail semiannual newsletter on trends in color, fashion, wardrobing, career dressing, party dressing, and skin care. Offer gift certificates, workshops, and drawing for free consultation. Send press releases stressing benefits of consultation; offer free pamphlet to readers.

Clothing alteration: Yellow Pages ad; quarterly flyer to clients offering special prices; ask for referrals; contact apparel shops for referrals.

Craft shop: Yellow Pages ad. Schedule workshops and classes; mail notices to customers and press releases to media. Offer in-store assistance.

Dentist: Call each patient every six months to arrange for check up appointment; mail semiannual newsletter on care and cleaning of the teeth, and latest discoveries in dentistry.

Dog & Cat Grooming: Phone or mail reminder cards for grooming. Send quarterly newsletter on pet care, i.e., diet, allergy, skin conditions, and importance of grooming. Invite customers to in-store workshop.

Fabric shop: Hold classes, workshops, and in-store promotions. Issue punch cards for give-away when completed; send quarterly newsletter with specials, fabric care and sewing updates. Send press releases.

Florist: Send pamphlets to churches, wedding consultants, caterers, clubs, and restaurants. Hold yearly open house, demonstrating decorating techniques for holidays, weddings, etc.

Gift shop: Offer punch card for give-away; gift wrapping and cards; delivery service; in-store instruction on repair of china, dolls, figurines, etc.

Gunsmith: Send yearly letter to clients; offer special price on pre/postseason cleaning and inspection; prepare pamphlet on business to hand out; ask for referrals from current clients.

Health food store: Send quarterly newsletter stressing importance of nutrition to health; hold classes or seminars featuring speakers on subject. Mail press releases as well as invitations to clients.

Hobby shop: Hold classes, workshops; send press releases to media and flyers to customers; Take special orders and notify by phone; offer in-store free advice; organize a club, hold meetings.

Insurance broker: Send quarterly newsletter with updates on insurance requirements, laws, etc. Phone twice yearly, and especially prior to renewal. Explain policy coverages, how client can save, and offer financing.

Knife & scissors sharpening: Visit fabric and hardware stores; schedule a weekly date to collect/deliver sharpened items. Leave business cards, flyers at sewing machine stores (by permission).

Knitting machine store: Hold in-store promotions as well as malls and craft shows; send press releases to local weekly papers about upcoming workshops, classes, seminars; send newsletters to customers advising what's new in yarns, designs, techniques and urging them to attend a workshop.

Limo service: *Prepare brochure to handout/mail to wedding consultants, high school prom committee, Bed & Breakfasts, Promo Director for shopping malls and tourist and convention bureaus. Volunteer   limo service to visiting dignitaries.*

Landscaping: *Prepare pamphlet stressing benefits of professional landscaping and care; leave with likely prospect, at garden centers and hardware stores (by permission), offer free estimates, make cold calls or leave pamphlets; contact home builders for referrals.*

Multi-level-marketing: *Send newsletters monthly; updates on products and product information; monthly discounts; bonus programs; meeting schedules, etc.*

Musician: *Hand out business cards to everyone. Prepare brochures and get to churches, associations, clubs, restaurants with banquet facilities. Consider Yellow Pages ad or local weekly to pick up family reunions, class reunions, etc.*

Photography: *Specialize in subject matter:reunions, family; weddings; pets; commercial product; passports; charter trips; parties. Hand out lots of business cards; prepare brochure showing sample of work.*

Printer: *Give lots of service. Offer help with layout and pasteup, photocopy machine for customer use, pick up and delivery service, notify regular customers of price increases ahead of time. Keep quality top notch and prices competitive.*

Restaurant: *Give lots of service! Offer punch card incentive, senior citizen discounts, catering, banquet room, meeting room. Notify clubs and associations.*

Rubber stamps: *Send semiannual brochure stressing capabilities, service. Solicit banks for "endorsement stamp" business on new accounts. Yellow Pages ad.*

Saw sharpening: *Contact retailers of equipment you sharpen; supply with certificates good for one free* *sharpening; leave business card with hardware stores, landscapers, wood cutters, saw shops, etc.*

Sales rep: *Manufacturer's representatives will have monthly or seasonal contact with buyers. Mail flyer or brochure advising new products, followed by phone call to make appointment.*

Vitamins: *Send monthly newsletter with update on product knowledge. Phone monthly for order or motivate with coupons in newsletter.*

Upholstery: *Yellow Pages ad. Mail flyer semiannually advising trends in colors and fabrics, offering special prices, and asking for referrals. Follow up each job 30 days later by phoning to ask if satisfactory. Mail flyer and business card three months later.*

NOTE TO THE READER: The above are given as suggestions only, and no inference is intended that some more than others should take advertising in the <u>Yellow Pages</u>. You are encouraged to adapt the suggestions as necessary, or enter your own ideas!

"If it weren't for the last minute, nothing would get done."

author unknown

What is a press release? It's a newsworthy bit of information sent to a newspaper or radio program in hopes of getting mentioned at no charge, with the end result of bringing attention to your business. It is also called a "news release."

You can spot press releases in your local paper by finding articles that mention local businesses--events, promotions, new locations or services offered, awards received or an employee's retirement--all are typical press release information. You can believe that the newspaper "got wind" of it because of a press release sent by the business itself.

Press releases benefit both the newspaper (free news copy and hopes of securing paid advertising at a later date), and the business (free exposure to possible new customers).

With a little creativity, you can turn almost anything into a press release. A few newsworthy reasons to send a press release are: a donation to a public institution or fund raising drive (money or merchandise), giving a workshop, a class, a lecture, or starting a school, creating a new recipe, inventing a helpful household hint, writing a letter to the editor, or donating instruction to a prison, nursing home, or hospital. Carole Katchen gives a lengthy list in her book *Promoting and Selling Your Art* (Watson Guptill Publications, 1978).

To whom is a press release mailed? To determine where your best audience is--the readers that would be likely to respond to your news--study local newspapers for advertising and printed press releases. What type of "news" are they likely to print? What types of advertising do they accept? What type of person reads that paper? The advertising will tell you. Would those readers be likely candidates for your product or services? If so, then write down the newspaper name, mailing address, and the name of the editor in charge of the section your press release would most likely appear in. If you're sending news of a new automobile tire or a new line of tennis racquets, aim for the sports section. Likewise, if the paper uses a lot of cigarette ads, don't expect the editor to print your news release on an antismoking meeting. But you can try!

Another thing you can do is scan the *Yellow Pages* under Newspapers and Radio Stations for addresses and phone numbers of the ones you would like to contact. Then call each one, requesting the name of the person or managing editor in charge of your target section: the sports editor, the business and finance editor, or the women's editor, and so on.

Ask also what the "closing" or "deadline" day is for the following week's paper. If it is a daily paper, forget the deadline and just mail it in (see **When should it be mailed?** later in this section).

Press releases addressed to a specific editor, by name, must be mailed without delay. There is a great turnover in editors in the publishing world, and if the one you addressed has moved on, your press release may be discarded without even opening the envelope!

Another place to find names of newspapers and magazines is *Writer's Market,* a listing of publishers printed yearly by Writer's Digest. You can find a current copy in the public library.

Also in the library is *The Literary Market Place,* which lists papers and radio and television stations nationwide. It should be in the reference section; ask the librarian for help if you cannot find it.

When should a press release be mailed? To know when to send a press release, you will have to understand "lead" time. That is the time a newspaper or magazine needs to review, edit, and typeset your press release before printing it in a particulat issue. Your press release must be sent well ahead of time, and you can determine a mailing date by using a calendar.

Suppose you are holding an in-store promotion on Saturday, June 19th, and decide to send press releases to two local weekly papers which are delivered on Wednesdays. The Wednesday before your promotion is June 16th, the paper you will want the release to be in. The closing date for the weekly paper is every Friday, so your press release must be received by the editor no later than June 11th.

Allow an extra day for delivery, and mail your press release on Wednesday, June 9th. That will give the paper sufficient time for editing and typesetting. You should know that magazines often have a lead time of three months or more.

Must press releases by typewritten? In a word— Yes! See the sample that follows for form: headings, margins, and spacing. One school of thought is that each press release should be original type; however, because you will be sending several, a good clean clear photocopy should work as well.

Use crisp, white, 8½"x11" paper (never colored). Don't use erasable paper as it tends to smear when handled by as many people as your press release will be.

Letterhead, or company stationery, is acceptable for press releases. There are those who feel that the letterhead detracts from the message of the press release and those who feel it adds credibility. If you choose to use it, leave at least two inches below the actual letterhead to begin your press release.

I prefer plain, crisp, white paper, 20 pound, 25% cotton fiber, with the company name and address typed at the bottom, below the name of the contact person.

Whichever you choose, use a clean, very black ribbon (film or carbon ribbon is best, but use what you have). Type on one side only, double spaced. Keep abbreviations to a minimum to avoid misunderstanding, and write out single digit numbers, like **two** rather than **2**. Numerals may be used for multiple digit numbers, like **22**, and for dates **July 22, 1987,** and for the time of day **2:00 P.M.** and for amounts of money, **$22.00.**

You can enclose a reply card, postage paid, asking if the press release will be used and when, but don't push your luck! They know what you're after, and at what price!

Is there a formula for writing a press release?
There is a kind of formula for writing press releases.
Don't write to tell them you are selling Bottled Body
Odor for $10.00 a bottle. That's an ad, and you
must pay for it.

Remember that you are writing a news or press
release, so your reason must be (1) newsworthy, or
seem that way. You will want to indicate a (2)
benefit to the reader, to (3) create interest in your
business and (4) motivate readers to seek you out,
which means your (5) business name, location, and
phone must be included.

Mention any (6) unusual specifics about your
product or service without becoming high-tech, and
(7) include dates, times, and the cost to the reader.

It doesn't hurt to work in a (8) short biography
of yourself; when the business was started; its goals
and purpose (to benefit the customer, of course).
Start with the most important news item first, and
decrease to the least important. That way, if the
editor has limited space, the least important
information is the most likely to be cut.

You must also give your name and phone number
as a contact person, and indicate that you are
available and willing to be questioned. This often
leads to an interview!

Analysis of a press release: In the sample press
release that follows, you will note that in the very
first sentence, Wally has (1) given the business
name, location, (2) given credibility to his business
by showing how long he's been established, (3) given
the day and time of the event, and (4) provided
motivation by limiting the time.

His second sentence gives the reader (5) two
benefits (free samples and 40% savings) as well as
(6) pointing out an unusual aspect (new flavor) and
(7) letting readers know what he does in addition
to wedding cakes!

The third sentence expands on his capabilities and
lets readers know his work is unique. Readers begin
to visualize a cake that matches the color scheme of
the wedding.

The last sentence is a short "bio." It gives

Wally's qualifications and makes the reader identify with the "home town boy."

Recipients of the press release can easily contact Wally for more information, verification, or to request an interview. Note that his full name, address, and phone number appear at the bottom as "contact person." Wally has added an informal, personal touch by individually signing each press release.

# # #

May 1, 1988

FOR IMMEDIATE RELEASE

Wally's Cakes on Promise Avenue at Lace Street will celebrate its 12th anniversary on Saturday, May 13th, with an open house from 2:00 to 4:00 PM.

Samples of a new flavor in wedding cakes, orange-coconut, will be offered along with free coffee and a 40% savings on all orders for cake top ornaments.

Wally's also designs birthday and retirement cakes, but is especially known for wedding cakes with buttercream roses tinted to match the wedding flowers and attendants' dresses.

Wally studied at the Paris School of Pastrie' and served as dessert chef for Chicago Cakes before returning home to Arbortown, where he started Wally's Cakes.

# # #

FOR MORE INFORMATION CONTACT:

Wally Bygolly

Wally Bygolly
3323 Promise Avenue
Arbortown, USA 33323
(555)123-4567

---

*The foregoing was excerpted from the book **HOW TO MAKE NEWSLETTERS, BROCHURES, & OTHER GOOD STUFF WITHOUT A COMPUTER SYSTEM,** by H. Gregory.

The "###" following the press release indicate "the end" of copy to the editor/publisher.

Plan in advance what day is best for mailing your press release.

JUNE						
SUN	MON	TUE	WED	THU	FRI	SAT
		1	2	3	4	5
6	7	8	9	10	11	12
13	14	15	16	17	18	19
20	21	22	23	24	25	26
27	28	29	30			

What is a newsletter? A newsletter is a gathering of product information and relative news, mailed to your customers and potential customers on a regular basis. The writing style is informal, much like writing to a friend.

A newsletter can be from one to several pages in length. It should not be entirely sales or promotional in nature, and because of the informative content, is often saved or passed on to others to read. That increases your readership and exposure!

You will note, when obtaining "media kits" from magazines, that circulation figures often are based on "readership" rather than actual "paid circulation."

Why should you send one? The purpose of your newsletter is to inform your customers about products or services, and to motivate them to buy.

You'll need to send newsletters AT LEAST four times per year if you don't want your customer to forget your existence. Most newsletters are sent monthly--schedule yours according to how often your product or service needs renewing (more often if you want to introduce and promote new products).

Newsletters are increasingly popular with small business owners, as they discover that direct mail to a "target" audience brings results! "Advertising can be valuable," reports the Small Business Administration in its publication **Marketing for Small Business**, "but in many cases advertisements in newspapers, television, etc., are too expensive for small businesses. Direct mail to key customers is frequently suggested."

How much will it cost? To figure out the costs, you'll have to make some decisions: what size paper will you use? Colored or white? Will you design "self-mailers" or use envelopes? First class mail or bulk?

I suggest starting with a single page newsletter, 8½X11, printed on both sides. If you have a small mailing list (100-200), photocopying will be satisfactory, and you can mail in envelopes at first class postage.

Shop the discount-paper stores for envelopes by the box (500). These can run from $6.00 to $16.00 per box. Shop and compare!

Same for copying or printing costs. Shop and compare! Use your telephone to get prices and return time (how long it takes to be printed). Consider convenience of location as well--a shop across town where parking is difficult may cost you more in time and gasoline than a closer shop charging only a cent or two more per copy.

Postage will cost you the same at any Post Office! Bulk mail can come into play when you have in excess of 200 pieces of mail exactly the same. Ask to talk to the Bulk Mail Clerk at your Post Office.

There is a yearly fee for the bulk mail permit, which is good only for the calendar year--if you buy the permit in October, it still expires on December 31st! Know that you will do all the zip code sorting, bundling, labeling, and hauling to the post office yourself.

If you don't want to address your newsletters by hand, ask for a "master sheet" for Avery labels at your quick-print shop. You can type or print your address list once and have it photocopied onto a sheet of 33 self-stick labels for about 35¢.

Add it all up for your total costs: printing and paper, envelopes, address labels, and postage.

Where do you start? My first suggestion would be to get a copy of my first small-business book: **How to make Newsletters, Brochures, & Other Good Stuff without a computer system.** In it you'll discover detailed steps to take you "from the blank page to the finished product." It includes information on supplies, layout and design, writing promotional copy, reproducing photographs with good results, and much more that room will not allow here. The book might be available at your library (if not, ask your library to buy one) or you can order it from a bookstore, or from the publisher of this book.

Here are the basics:

1. Graphic supplies. You'll need white paper, black marking pens (medium and fine point; dense black), pencils, eraser, stick glue (waxy type) or rubber cement, a twelve inch ruler, a scissors, and maybe a pad of tracing paper. Your "camera ready" original (also called a "pasteup" or "mechnical") is ALWAYS black ink on white paper, no matter what color paper you'll have it printed on. Get white paper that will not allow your black pens to "bleed" (fuzz out from the original line).

2. Artwork. Artwork is any drawing, illustration, or photographs to be used on your pasteup. They too must be black and white. For starters, use only illustrations, black on white paper, which might be obtained from your supplier or a clip art source book (ask at the graphic supply store). Show your product in use, or the benefit of its use.

EXAMPLE: The tired homemaker with aching feet, finding relief in velvety slippers (your product).

EXAMPLE: The sleepy eyed executive, coming alive by sipping a special blend of afternoon-herbal tea (your product).

EXAMPLE: Weary, snow-covered travellers, finding a mellow fire, warm chocolate, and a feather-bed in (your) Bed & Breakfast Inn.

3. Product Information. Use the same information you found in Section One of this book: your research. Just as in your sales presentation, you'll want to stress benefits in your newsletter.

4. Dummy copy. Make a pencil sketch, using paper the same size as your finished newsletter, showing placement of artwork (illustrations) and copy (text). BE SURE your name, address, and phone is included!

5. Write copy. Write your newsletter copy, beginning with a "hook" (major benefit), into the "body" (specifics like size, colors, availability, price) and on to the "close" or "call to action" (motivate reader to buy. Tell your reader what to do, "pick up the phone," "cut out the coupon," "Send in the order." Also include timely "news" relative to your product or service. This can be clippings from product brochures, paraphrases of newspaper or magazine articles, or quotes from satisfied customers.

6. Typeset and Pasteup. Your copy can be "typeset" by typewriter or hand printing on white paper. Using your dummy layout as a guide, "typeset" copy to fit the spaced around your artwork.

Leave a quarter of an inch on all four sides of your pasteup paper (layout sheet), and also a small margin around artwork and sections of copy. Apply glue stick or rubber cement to the back of the copy, and position in place, pressing only slightly to maintain placement. When all your pieces have been positioned, cover the pasteup with a blank sheet of paper or tracing paper, and burnish (rub down) firmly with a small ruler or the spine of a book. Edges must be firmly attached, and there should be no wrinkles in your pasteup.

Make a separate pasteup sheet for each side or page to be printed.

7. Get it printed! Slip your pasteup into a large envelope or file folder to keep it smudge-free.

8. Mail it! When your newsletters are done, you will have to fold, address (envelopes or labels), add postage, sort, and mail.

1.

RESEARCH

PROSPECTING →

2.

MAKING
APPOINTMENTS

3.

THE BUSINESS CYCLE

From product research to customer search to making appointments to giving the presentation, to closing the sale, to following up sales and leads, to repeat sales and referrals.

4.

GIVING THE SALES
PRESENTATION

8.

REFERRALS

Dear Customer,
Thank you for your order. It will be delivered next Tuesday.
I'll call you in a couple of weeks to see how you like it!

6.

← FOLLOW-UP

7.

REPEAT
SALES

5.

CLOSING THE SALE

INDEX

A

Accessories 10
Advertising 48, 121
Alphabet 16, 17
Answering machine 54
Appointments, making, 54, 55
Appointments, example of, 58, 59
Approach 34
Arm yourself 3
Articles 37
Attainable, goals, 27
Attitude 19-22
Associations 105

B

Background, self, 34, 37
Baseball players 46
Beecher, Henry Ward 70
Benefits 32, 33, 34
Bibliography 7
Blank paper 33
Body language 17-19, 41
Body, writing, 32, 33, 41, 55
Books 106-109
"Break-the-ice" goal 27
Bulges and fabric, 14
Bulletin boards 48
Business cards 47, 49
Business cycle 139
Business suit 9
Business wardrobe 10, 11
Brochures 47, 49

C

Calendar 27
Call-to-action 32, 33
Cards, 3x5, 77
Chamber of Commerce 93, 94
Chase's Calendar of Annual Events 51
Cheerful 19
Children 24
Children and telephone 60
Clarity of voice 15
Classes 49, 77, 101, 110
Close of presentation 19, 32, 33, 37, 41
Clothing design 14
Club, start, 49
Colors 9, 10, 13
Color analysis 13-15
Color combinations 13
Column, write a, 50
Commission 29
Commercials 9
Competition 6, 23, 39, 41

Complaints, customer, 91
Complexion 13
Conduct 20
Consultant, color & wardrobe, 13, locate 14
Contests, hold, 49
Convictions, in product, 34
Customer field test 82-83
Customer service 82
Customer type 46

D

Dewey Decimal System 116
Diagonal lines 14
Direct mail 47
Directories 47
Dogmatic 34
Door-to-door 49
Do's & Don't's 67-69
"Dream Boards" 28
Drop-in customers 52
Dues 23, 41

E

Earrings 10
Ears 30
Eat out 50
Employees 49, 85
Endorsements 37
Enthusiastic 20
Enunciate 15
Eye contact 19, 31, 40, 63

F

Fabrics 10, 13, 14
Face-to-face 62
Family 46
Fan mail 22
"Feeling Blue?" 22
Feelings, create, 34
Figure 9
Financing 37
Finding, customers, 46
Flexible 50, 55
Flower garden 45, 92
Flynn, Errol 7
Flyers 30, 47, 48, 49
Follow up 47, 73-97
Follow up suggestions 123
Follow up system 77-81
Forbes, Malcolm 24
Friends 46
Full length mirror 8, 18

G

Garage sales 47
Garden, flower, 45
Gestures 18
Goal Sheet 26

Goals, setting 25, 74-75
Golden Rule 86
Group presentation 64

H

Hair color 13
Hairdressers 46
Handling objections 39
Handshake 18, 19
Hearing 31
Hearing impairments 16
Horizontal lines 14
"Hot button" 63

I

Identify, customers, 45, 46
Identify, self, 55
Income 29
Indifference 20
Interruptions 32
Introduction 32, 33, 41
In-store promotions 48

J

Jewelry 10

K

Keeping customers 73
Kids 24
Knowledge is power 5

L

Lant, Jeffrey 50, 51
Lapel pins 11
Lasch, Christopher 8
Leads 47
Leisure hours 23
Library 6, 15, 41, 47, 48
Library of Congress 116
Library research guide 113-119
Lips, read, 16
Listen 30, 31

M

Magazine 15, 110
Magazine, trade, 48
Mail order 66
Mailing, goals, 30, list 50
Makeup 13
Manufacturer 41
Mask, cardboard, 11
Media kit 101, 103
Merit pins 11
Mini presentation 54
Mirror 8, 18, 40, 41
Misunderstanding 16
Money 9, 27
Motivate, signs, 28, 37, 41
Multi-level marketing 28

N

N.G.R. 26
Need, customer, 20
Need, for product, 37
New residents 47
Newsletters 75, 76, 111
Newsletters, making of, 135
Newspaper 15, 48
Numbers, matter of, 46, 48
Numeral pronunciation 16

O

Objections 32, 37, 39, 41
Objection, sample of, 38
Objectivity, self, 8
Office furniture 23
Office hours 84
Organize, goals, 27

P

Parton, Dolly 20
Paying dues 23-25
Personal appearance 8, 41
Philosophy 34
Piggy bank 29
Pitch, voice, 15
Place, for work, 24
Planning 25
Policy 85, 87, 97
Positive 20
Postpone 23
Posture 18
Power colors 9, 13
Practice! 40
Press release 49, 129
Primary colors 13
Primetime 39
Product research 5, 32, 41
Professional coaching, voice, 17
Professional coaching, colors, 14
Prospecting 23
Pulling weeds 92
Public library 6, 41, 47
Public places 47
Public records 48
Publicity 49
Publish booklet 49

Q

Qualify, customer, 51
Qualified 34, 37
Quality, voice, 15
Quantity, voice, 15

R

Radio announcer 16
Recipe 31

Referrals 47
Reflection on attitude 21
Research 23
Research, library, 6, 113-119
Research, television, 9
Respect 19
Right to make money 9
Rosters 50
Rough draft 32

S

SASE 102
Sales presentation 16, 20, 31, 40, 41
Sales presentation, giving of, 61-69
Sales presentation, sample of, 35-36
Sample 47
Seating 19
Self image 41
Self manufacture 5, 25
Seminars 110
Senses, in selling, 62
Setting goals 25
Sequence of benefits 37
Shakespeare, Wm 12
Shorts 10
Sincere 19
Skin care 13
Smile 18
Speed, of voice, 15
Specific, goals, 27, 30
Standing to greet 18
Strangers 46
Subconscious 20, 28
Success, measured, 29
Supplier 41
Suppliers, office, 112
Supplies 61
Swim suits 10

T

Tape recorder 8, 15, 16, 40, 41
Teach a class 49
Telephone books 47
Telephone calls 56, 57
Telephone campaign 52, example of, 53
Telephone presentations 65
Telephone time table 56
Thank you 33, 76
Time 34
Tone, of voice, 15
Trade magazines 7, 48
Training, employees, 85
Training, kids, friends, 24
Travelogue narrator 16

U

Undertones, color, 13
Uniform, business, 8

Uniform, wealth, 9
Urgency 33

V

Value 32, 55
Vertical lines 14
Visions, create, 34
Visualizing, 20
Vocal instrument, 17
Voice analysis 15-17, 41
Voice exercises 15, 16, 17
Voice, volume, 15
Volunteer 50

W

Wages 29
Wardrobe, business, 10, 11
Wardrobe planning 9
Whisper 16
Words 34
Workplace 24
Workshop 49, 77
Write a column 50
Writing the sales presentation 31

Y

Yard sales 47
Yellow Pages 14
"Yes Mode" 33